I thank God that he
lets me be an atheist.

C. G. Lichtenberg

"Is there life after death?" is a nonsense question, but people will not stop asking it.

Raymond Moody

The slozy begoners floofed in tarkly from below in their cluddering, plaggering flootiedopters.

MAKING SENSE
OF NONSENSE

About the Author

Raymond Moody (Birmingham, AL) coined the term "near-death experience" in his *New York Times* best-selling book *Life After Life*. Throughout his five-decade career, he has publicly lectured about near-death and shared-death experiences, and he has published several best-selling books. He is a frequent television guest, having appeared dozens of times on national programs such as the *Oprah Winfrey Show*.

RAYMOND MOODY MD, PhD

MAKING SENSE OF NONSENSE

THE LOGICAL BRIDGE BETWEEN SCIENCE & SPIRITUALITY

LLEWELLYN PUBLICATIONS
WOODBURY, MINNESOTA

FIRST EDITION
First Printing, 2020

Book design by Rebecca Zins
Cover design by Shira Atakpu

Llewellyn Publications is a registered trademark
of Llewellyn Worldwide Ltd.

The Library of Congress Cataloging-in-Publication Data
Names: Moody, Raymond A., Jr., author.
Title: Making sense of nonsense : the logical bridge between science &
   spirituality / Raymond Moody.
Description: First edition. | Woodbury, Minnesota : Llewellyn Publications,
   2020. | Includes bibliographical references. | Summary: "In this book
   Dr. Moody shares the groundbreaking results of four decades of research
   into the philosophy of nonsense, revealing new ways to understand and
   experience life, death, and spirituality"—Provided by publisher.
Identifiers: LCCN 2019039230 (print) | LCCN 2019039231 (ebook) | ISBN
   9780738763163 (paperback) | ISBN 9780738763378 (ebook)
Subjects: LCSH: Meaninglessness (Philosophy) | Language and
   languages—Philosophy. | Nonsense literature—History and criticism. |
   Religion and science.
Classification: LCC B825.2 .M66 2020 (print) | LCC B825.2 (ebook) | DDC
   121—dc23
LC record available at https://lccn.loc.gov/2019039230
LC ebook record available at https://lccn.loc.gov/2019039231

Llewellyn Publications
A Division of Llewellyn Worldwide Ltd.
2143 Wooddale Drive
Woodbury, MN 55125-2989
www.llewellyn.com

Printed in the United States of America

Contents

Exercise List

*Wherever you come near the
human race, there's layers
and layers of nonsense.*

Thornton Wilder, *Our Town*

Introduction

> *To appreciate nonsense requires*
> *a serious interest in life.*
>
> Frank Gelett Burgess

Since 1965 I have interviewed thousands of people about their profound near-death experiences. In 1975 I published *Life After Life*, a book about my research, which sold more than twenty million copies all around the world, so I am known to the public mainly as a psychiatrist who studies life after death. Life after death is among the biggest questions of human existence, and many people take the subject very seriously, for it touches on strong, deep, heartfelt feelings that affect almost everybody. *Why, then*, they ask me, *did you write this book about nonsense?*

Nonsense and the idea of a life after death may seem far, far apart. In reality, however, you can't have one without the

1

other. Nonsense turns out to be the missing piece that always before blocked serious investigation of the afterlife. This book supplies the missing piece in the form of a new way of thinking about things that are nonsensical and unintelligible. Therefore, this book is also a major breakthrough on genuine rational inquiry into life after death. Let me explain.

When I was a child, my favorite subject was astronomy and my favorite authors were Dr. Seuss and Lewis Carroll. I spent lots of my free time gazing through a telescope and reading *Alice in Wonderland* and *Horton Hears a Who*. As a budding astronomer, I soon realized that the universe we live in doesn't make perfect sense. For instance, what size is the universe? Surely it comes to an end somewhere in some kind of wall. But doesn't there have to be something on the other side of a wall? The only other possibility, though, seems to be that the universe goes infinitely into outer space, with no end, and that makes no sense either.

When I was about eight years old, I realized that we live enclosed in a shimmering sphere of unintelligible nonsense. Meanwhile, Dr. Seuss, Edward Lear, and Lewis Carroll convinced me that nonsense is something truly wonderful. We are not confined to saying meaningful things like "The dog is sleeping peacefully by the fire" or "This hat costs thirty dollars" or "The moon is 240 thousand miles from the earth."

We can also say things like "Those five spumsy chaddlers almost plittered that little flifster into monunction" or "Holiness numerically sings the vestigial lipstick of spontaneity" or "That cannibal you men just ate was the last one in this county."

When I was about twelve years old, I realized that there are different types of nonsense, which later turned out to be a pivotal realization that shaped my thinking about near-death experiences. It served me well when I went to college and majored in philosophy, too, for nonsense is a core concept of Western philosophy, especially modern analytic philosophy. It was as a philosophy major reading Plato that I first encountered near-death experiences.

Early Greek philosophers understood full well that people sometimes report spiritual experiences when they are revived from close calls with death. Plato wrote about the famous case of a soldier who apparently died in battle but spontaneously revived at his funeral. The soldier told amazed spectators that he had left his body and went through a passageway into another world. Plato thought that such accounts indicated a transcendent world beyond death.

Another Greek philosopher, Democritus, thought differently about experiences like those. Democritus had figured out that things in the world are composed of minute, indivisible particles—atoms—that are too small to be seen. Democritus wrote that the experiences of people who recovered from apparent death were caused by residual biological activity in the body. He said that there is no such thing as a moment of death; dying is a process.

The debate about near-death experiences has not progressed much since then. Some claim that near-death experiences are evidence of life after death. Others claim that the experiences result from oxygen deprivation to the brain. This book explodes that old framework of debate by setting out an entirely new way of thinking. Specifically, this book solves the primary problem that previously prevented real advances toward answering the question of life after death.

David Hume (1711–1776) was a renowned philosopher who refined our concepts of causation and inductive reasoning. His famous skeptical works helped shape what we know as the scientific mind. In an incisive analysis, Hume pinpointed the real problem of inquiring into the afterlife. Hume said,

> By the mere light of reason it seems difficult to prove the Immortality of the Soul...Some new species of logic is requisite for that purpose, and some new faculties of the mind that they may enable us to comprehend that logic.[1]

Hume was right. In reality, we can't solve the afterlife problem with the logic we have and the mind we have. The logic you are using right now as you read this is based on literal meaning. In that logic, "There is life after death" is a self-contradiction. After all, "death" just means "the final, irreversible cessation of life." Hence, saying that "there is life

---

1   Hume, *Essays and Treatises on Various Subjects*, 226, 229.

after the final, irreversible cessation of life" is just meaningless.

This book solves Hume's problem by setting out a new logic—a logic of nonsense. Learning these new rational principles will actually activate previously hidden powers of your mind. At the end of this book, all these new logical principles and new powers of the mind will come together. Then we will be able to shine astonishing new light on life after death and other big questions of science and religion.

After a stint as a philosophy professor, I went to medical school. I soon noticed that patients who were delirious, intoxicated, psychotic, severely stressed, or confused often talked nonsense. Moreover, when ill patients talked nonsense involuntarily, they talked the same types of nonsense that authors like Dr. Seuss and Lewis Carroll wrote deliberately. That is, nonsense is nonsense whether it is deliberate or involuntary.

Eventually, I brought together all I had learned into a semester-length university course on nonsense, which I taught numerous times. Students learned about the many important psychological and spiritual effects of nonsense and the many roles nonsense plays in humor, songs, advertising, literature, religion, and the quest for knowledge. My students learned to recognize more than seventy different types of nonsense, describe their structures, and write their own examples.

Similarly, here you will learn about the nature of nonsense, its various forms, and why it is important. From there, we'll look at deep connections between nonsense and the mind to bring the hidden, unconscious world of nonsense fully into your conscious mind and better understand both the rules it follows and the rules it breaks. You'll also learn about the spiritual significance of nonsense and how it has appeared historically in sacred texts, ritual and magical practices, and tradition for inducing transcendent or mystical states of consciousness. Next we'll review the relationships between nonsense and our search for rational knowledge. In addition, we'll take a look at the important topic of misuses of nonsense and how it is sometimes used for manipulation and selfish purposes. And finally, with a clear foundation of nonsense set, we'll review the fascinating topic of how it plays a role in our understanding of life after death.

The students in my university course also completed nonsense exercises as part of their practice, which awakened unknown cognitive and creative powers of their minds. The exercises I designed for my courses are reprinted throughout chapter 2 in this book for your own practice. By completing them, you will find that you are able to think logically and creatively about questions that previously eluded reason, and you will attain a revolutionary new understanding of the mysteries of the next life.

Let's begin.

Chapter 1

THE NATURE OF NONSENSE

> *[Nonsense] is not a vacuity of*
> *sense; it is a parody of sense,*
> *and that is the sense of it.*
>
> T. S. Eliot

Nonsense is spoken, written, or signed language that is unintelligible because it is meaningless. That is the primary meaning of the term as it appears in standard dictionaries. Nonsense, to be nonsense, must be language, it must be unintelligible, and it must be meaningless. All three are necessary to fit the definition.

Nonsense is, first, language. We should not be misled by the common expression "Stop your nonsense!" Saying "Stop your nonsense!" signals the speaker's strong disapproval of another person's nonverbal, extralinguistic behavior. Nonverbal behavior, since it is not language, is not nonsense in the dictionary meaning of the term. For example, admonishing subordinates for their nonverbal actions and extralinguistic misbehavior is only a secondary, extended use of the word nonsense.

Nonsense is, secondly, unintelligible. Saying that something is unintelligible means that it cannot be comprehended by the intellect; in other words, something that is unintelligible is beyond the reach of the intellectual or rational mind. We cannot wrap our minds around something that is unintelligible. For language to be nonsense, then, it must be unintelligible.

Sometimes people say that something is unintelligible because they personally cannot comprehend it. People who cannot speak Chinese, for example, might sometimes say that Chinese is unintelligible. By saying that, though, they are acknowledging a personal limitation: specifically, an inability to speak Chinese. Generally they know full well that Chinese is a meaningful language that is intelligible to the people who speak it.

People may sometimes talk loosely and say, for example, that the writing in an old, faded letter is unintelligible. By saying that, they would mean only that time obliterated so much of the original writing that the message cannot be recovered. Or they might mean that the writer's penmanship is so terrible that the writing is illegible and the message unreadable. Generally, though, they would assume that there was a meaningful message in the letter when the writer originally wrote it.

Nonsense, however, is language that is unintelligible because it is, thirdly, meaningless. In other words, nonsense is language that does not make sense because the words or sentences do not fit together to convey a coherent meaning. In sum, then, nonsense is meaningless, unintelligible language.

Now, I want to make something crystal clear from the very beginning about that word *meaningless*. Specifically, nonsense is meaningless only in the context of its linguistic meaning, for nonsense is deeply meaningful to people in a multitude of ways. Nonsense plays important roles in children's literature, music, psychology, religion, and the spiritual life. This book is full of instances of the rich meanings nonsense has for us in those dimensions of our lives.

Nonsense lacks linguistic meaning, to be sure, but a linguistic meaning is something we can look up in a dictionary. The other rich meanings nonsense has for us are found in our hearts and minds and souls.

Therefore, whenever I say that nonsense is meaningless, I am referring only to its lack of a linguistic dictionary meaning. Throughout this book, we will celebrate how meaningful nonsense is in our lives, while fully understanding it is devoid of linguistic meaning.

Nonsense can be deliberate or involuntary. People sometimes write or talk nonsense on purpose. They include, for example, nonsense poets or other writers who create nonsense as an art form. Those writers work deliberately and diligently to produce entertaining or aesthetically pleasing works that are meaningless and unintelligible.

People also sometimes deliberately talk nonsense for fraud or imposture. In 2014 a fake sign language interpreter stood beside President Obama on the speakers' platform at the memorial for Nelson Mandela. As the president and other dignitaries spoke, the impostor flapped his arms and gesticulated wildly in what was supposedly sign language for the deaf, yet deaf people who watched could not make sense of what the sign language interpreter was saying. The impostor's entire "interpretation" was meaningless nonsense.

An expert on sign language said that the impostor's hand positions were meaningless. The expert also pointed out that the impostor did not "use facial expressions, head movements, shoulder-raising or other body language considered integral elements of signing." Authorities were unable to determine how the fake interpreter got through security to talk nonsense next to the president of the United States.

Other times people talk nonsense involuntarily. That is, they talk nonsense without intending to; in other words, they sometimes lapse unknowingly into saying something that is meaningless and unintelligible. For example, people sometimes talk nonsense involuntarily because of a certain medical or psychological condition. Specifically, people who are psychotic, delirious, intoxicated, asleep, or having a stroke or a migraine sometimes talk unintelligible nonsense involuntarily.

People sometimes talk nonsense without intending to simply because of a conceptual confusion. That is, they unwittingly get concepts mixed up, and hence, they say something that is meaningless and unintelligible. Nonsense that comes from conceptual confusion occurs in people from all walks of life. For example, a highly successful coach once said to his team, "You guys line up alphabetically by height."

Nonsense that results from inadvertent conceptual confusion is of particular interest to analytic philosophers. Bertrand Russell, Ludwig Wittgenstein, and Gilbert Ryle were among early analytic philosophers who argued that many traditional philosophical problems are meaningless, unintelligible nonsense. That was the central tenet of analytic philosophy.

Now, people who talk nonsense because of a physical or mental illness are often in a clouded state of consciousness. People who talk nonsense when they are half asleep, delirious, or crazy, for example, are not fully alert or may be only semiconscious. They may talk nonsense from within a strange dreamlike state in which they are unable to draw distinctions; in that state they cannot think logically or coherently.

In contrast, people who are working on philosophical problems are typically fully alert and in a lucid state of consciousness. Philosophical questions are difficult and tricky to begin with, though, and it is easy for even careful, logical thinkers to get confused. When their conceptual confusions are pointed out to them, they usually realize that they were talking nonsense and adjust their thinking. In contrast, delirious, intoxicated, or psychotic patients cannot comprehend that they are talking nonsense, nor can they adjust their thinking.

Nonsense can be deliberate or involuntary, and involuntary nonsense is common in hospitals, especially psychiatric hospitals. Doctors and nurses working in those settings frequently hear their patients talking nonsense involuntarily. Far more people are out and about than are working in hospitals, though, and those people are far more likely to hear or read nonsense that someone created deliberately, usually for entertainment or artistic purposes.

Nonsense is predominantly a recreational and literary form of language. The nonsense that most Americans hear or read most frequently was written for use in play, recreation, entertainment, literature, and songs. Nonsense is common in children's oral literature, such as nursery rhymes, jump rope rhymes, and riddles. Popular children's authors who are famous for their nonsense writings include Edward Lear, Lewis Carroll, Dr. Seuss, Quentin Blake, and Shel Silverstein. Authors such as Alfred Jarry and Samuel Beckett wrote surrealistic nonsense that provoked philosophical discussion among adult readers and theater audiences. To summarize, then, nonsense is a genre of oral and written literature for children and adults.

The next chapter will give specific examples of nonsense from all of the above authors. Later we will refer to some examples of nonsense from popular forms of music, too, for nonsense is a standard ingredient of certain kinds of songs, including traditional ballads, scat singing, and doo-wop. Nonsense in entertainment, recreation, play, poetry, and song is ubiquitous in modern American society. Moreover, those are the settings in which Americans most frequently encounter nonsense, and therefore, for them, nonsense is a thoroughly pleasant experience.

Still, people hardly ever think about all of the positive nonsense that they take in as nonsense. Strangely, it never occurs to them that, for instance, lines in popular songs they like to listen to are nonsense. Although nonsense they hear and read almost always affects them positively, and they like it, they seldom think of it as nonsense. In fact, the word "nonsense" has a strongly negative effect on them.

Nonsense itself affects people positively, but the word "nonsense" affects people negatively. That is, people like nonsense itself, but they dislike the word "nonsense." People do not associate the many good effects they enjoy from deliberate nonsense with the word "nonsense." Instead, they associate the word "nonsense" with one common negative effect of involuntary nonsense: specifically, errors.

"Nonsense" is predominantly a pejorative term of criticism and debate. Nonsense sometimes indicates a cognitive failure. Delirious, psychotic, or intoxicated people, as already noted, talk nonsense involuntarily because they have difficulty with cognitive processing. People whose cognitive processes are fully intact may, nonetheless, talk nonsense inadvertently because of mixing incompatible concepts. For example, a football coach once said to his players, "You guys pair up in threes."

In other words, talking nonsense without intending to is sometimes a sign of cognitive impairment due to organic illness or somebody may talk nonsense unintentionally because of misunderstanding concepts. Talking nonsense is a kind of error in both cases. Accordingly, people naturally associated talking nonsense with errors, and they then use the word "nonsense" pejoratively to denounce something somebody else said.

"Nonsense," "unintelligible," and "meaningless" are stock terms of criticism in serious scientific, academic, and religious debate. Saying "That is nonsense!" is an accepted way of objecting to new ideas that are put forward for rational inquiry. Objecting that an idea is unintelligible or meaningless or nonsensical is a common ploy in learned debate as well as in public discourse. In fact, the word "nonsense" occurs most frequently within the context of debate and disputation.

The following selection of quotations will illustrate how common this kind of objection is. The examples below are typical of many others that anyone could find. They are common in news magazines, newspapers, academic works, and science publications.

> Squeezing light—the very idea seems nonsensical. How do you grab something as intangible as light and throttle it down to something smaller? Understanding how

this is possible goes to the heart of what we now know light to be.

—*Sidney Perkowitz*[2]

People often criticize discussions of multiple universes as meaningless because we can't detect whether they actually exist.

—*Anthony Aquirre*[3]

Infinity mathematics, to me, is something that is meaningless, because it is abstract nonsense....We have to kick the misleading word "undecidable" from the mathematical lingo since it tacitly assumes that infinity is real. We should rather replace it with the phrase "not even wrong" (in other words, utter nonsense).

—*Doron Zeilberger*[4]

Some researchers believe that by writing and then editing our own stories, we can change our perceptions of ourselves and identify obstacles that stand in the way of better health. It may sound like self-help nonsense, but research suggests that the effects are real.

—*Tara Parker-Pope*[5]

2   Perkowitz, "Light Tricks."

3   Lifeboat Foundation, "Advisory Board."

4   Zeilberger, "Opinion 108."

5   Parker-Pope, "Writing Your Way to Happiness."

> Some people might think of "miracles" as particular juxtapositions of events, each of which has a correct and acceptable scientific explanation. This might be nonsensical, but it would be interesting to discover wherein the nonsense lies.
>
> —*Hugh McLachlan*[6]

Evidently, dismissing somebody's ideas as "unintelligible nonsense" is an accepted technique of raising an objection in rational debate. Objections that some proposed idea is nonsense have been raised and debated in physics, cosmology, philosophy, mathematics, religious studies, medicine, and economics. The quotations above are enough to tell us a lot about the use of "nonsense" in rational argumentation and disputation.

Ancient Greek philosophers who founded rational thought dubbed ideas "nonsense" as a way of rejecting them and setting them aside. That way of arguing against inconvenient ideas or claims is still standard practice in the pursuit of knowledge. Furthermore, objecting that an unfamiliar notion is unintelligible nonsense is treated as though it were a powerful argument. After all, if a claim is unintelligible, there is nothing there in the way of content that can be investigated by rational methods. Theoretically, then, demonstrating that somebody's idea or position is unintelligible nonsense should put a stop to rational inquiry into the matter.

---

6   Novella, "New Scientist on Miracles."

When raising this kind of objection, people use "nonsense" and "unintelligible" and "meaningless" as interchangeable terms. Yet, despite the presumed authority and finality of proving that an idea is unintelligible and nonsensical, this form of argument has a poor track record. For centuries, scoffers have greeted revolutionary new thoughts and theories by saying that they are unintelligible or nonsensical.

There are no explicit, public rules and procedures that govern accusing someone of talking nonsense or defending one's own position against such an accusation. That is shocking, too, given that arguing that way is such a widespread, accepted practice in serious scientific, academic, and religious discussions. Why is such a startling departure from rigorous, rational standards allowed in this case?

Different individuals may disagree about whether or not a particular idea is unintelligible. One person may say that the idea is unintelligible nonsense while another person says that the idea makes perfect sense. Yet, because there are no public, agreed-upon rules governing these arguments, there is no standard, rational method for resolving disagreements about unintelligibility. We need a standard criterion for identifying unintelligible nonsense in disputed cases.

Edward Lear, Lewis Carroll, and Dr. Seuss worked deliberately and diligently to write meaningless, unintelligible nonsense. They and a few other authors are renowned for their literary nonsense, and their success shows that they studied the subject of unintelligible language closely. Therefore, we will select examples of deliberate nonsense to build our theory of nonsense, for we can be assured that they are bona fide instances of unintelligible nonsense.

Clear-cut, positively identified examples of deliberate nonsense would provide a standard for settling some disputes about unintelligibility. If the alleged nonsense exactly matched bona fide, standard examples of deliberate nonsense, that would definitively settle the disagreement. A curious fact about deliberate nonsense, in relation to involuntary nonsense, is germane to this potential rational method of resolving some disagreements concerning unintelligibility.

Nonsense occurs in the same patterns regardless of whether it is deliberate or involuntary. Some nonsense is produced deliberately by writers for literary or entertainment purposes or by impostors for the purpose of fraud. Some nonsense is produced involuntarily by people who are sleepy or ill or mentally disturbed. Some nonsense is produced inadvertently by cognitively intact, fully conscious people who get confused about concepts. Even so, the same structural patterns appear in nonsense whether it is produced deliberately or involuntarily. Furthermore, the same structural patterns appear in nonsense whether it is produced by an alert, conscious, creative person or by an impaired, ill, semiconscious person.

In childhood I read my favorite works of nonsense with interest and in detail. In Carl Barks's and Lewis Carroll's works, especially, it was obvious that there were different kinds of nonsense. I further developed my ideas about different kinds of nonsense as a graduate student, and then later as a professor of philosophy. That way, I worked out a preliminary system of nonsense types.

Afterwards, I studied medicine and became a medical doctor and psychiatrist. Throughout my studies and career in medicine and psychiatry, I paid attention when my physically ill, psychotic, cognitively impaired patients involuntarily talked or wrote nonsense. I found that my patients' involuntary nonsense was of the same type that creative writers produced deliberately. Apparently, therefore, nonsense has its own internal logic that operates, in part, independently of particular individuals' intentions, state of consciousness, or cognitive status.

I recognized all of the nonsense my patients talked or wrote from my studies of nonsense created deliberately by writers. However, I identified many types of deliberate nonsense in works by creative writers that I never recognized in the speech or writings of my patients. Therefore, it seems to me that creative, deliberate nonsense is fuller, richer, and more inclusive than involuntary nonsense associated with pathological states.

Nonsense is a valuable part of language that deserves serious study. Even so, some people resist the idea of rational studies of nonsense. What is the peculiar stigma that many people attach to unintelligible nonsense?

Nonsense is surrounded by several entrenched misconceptions, faulty assumptions, and half-truths. Most people have a bad attitude toward nonsense, and their bad attitude stems mostly from the strongly negative connotation of the pejorative word *nonsense*. People think nonsense is inherently bad and undesirable. They reflexively associate nonsense with emotions of disgust and repugnance. In their minds nonsense denotes a personal sense of displeasure and rejection. They assume that nonsense is an irredeemable, negative quantity with nothing good about it.

In reality, however, nonsense is part of the good life. Nonsense touches people's lives most frequently in play, entertainment, literature, and song. That repugnance most people feel toward nonsense is a case of mistaken identity. In real life, as we saw, nonsense is predominantly a recreational and literary department of language—and people love it.

Nonsense seems to be almost exclusively a good thing, yet a darker, obscure, preconscious force is at work in people's unrealistic attitude toward nonsense. Paul Davies touched on this darker irrational factor in a 2011 article in *New Scientist*: "The concept of a true void, apart from inducing a queasy feeling, strikes many people as preposterous or even meaningless."

People mistakenly think that nonsense is akin to nothingness, nonexistence, chaos, and the void. At the beginning of my courses, students completed an exercise that revealed the deep irrational connection between nonsense and nothingness. I asked students to define nonsense in their own words and to state what they think nonsense is. I also asked them to introspect, then describe their inner conscious and cognitive process of defining it.

As they reflected and tried to find the right words, many reported a similar image. They pictured nonsense as an impenetrable blank wall, and behind the wall, they imagined only a shapeless and empty chaos. For them, the word *nonsense* evoked a yawning abyss of undifferentiated darkness.

The recurrent, ancient image of nonsense as an inchoate nothingness is a frightening archetype. Thinking of nonsense can make people feel dizzy and disoriented. Socrates described the sensation when he was trying to think his way through a thicket of puzzling philosophical concepts. He said that the prospect of "falling into a bottomless pit of nonsense" horrified him (from Plato's *Parmenides*).

Most people regard nonsense as an absence of something else, namely, meaning. Few people think of nonsense as something in its own right. People think of nonsense as something sublinguistic, or as below the level of ordinary, meaningful language. In fact, *that* view sounds like common sense.

In reality, however, the relationship between nonsense and ordinary, meaningful language is the other way around. Nonsense is actually *above* the level of ordinary, meaningful language in a certain respect. Specifically, we shall see later that nonsense has a greater structural complexity than meaningful language. Therefore, nonsense is not akin to nothingness, and it is not merely the absence of meaning. Nonsense is a complex, extended form of language that operates by its own coherent inner logic. Therefore, nonsense is definitely not akin to nothingness, chaos, and the void.

Most people confuse nonsense with falsehood. That is, they do not distinguish between nonsense and falsehood. In fact, they think of nonsense as merely a particularly egregious or obnoxious form of falsehood. Nonsense is patently, blatantly a falsehood—even a falsehood with an exclamation point.

Equating nonsense with falsehood sounds like common sense, but nonsense is emphatically not the same thing as falsehood. In fact, as we shall see in chapter 6, nonsense and falsehood belong to two separate levels of reason and analysis. Furthermore, understanding the distinction between nonsense and falsehood is necessary for effective logical thinking about some major problems of philosophy, science, and religion. Chapter 7 will discuss the critical distinctions among truth, falsehood, and nonsense.

In class, I once saw a dark mood come over a bright student the first time I mentioned nonsense. When I asked why, she explained that nonsense made her think of madness, psychosis, and severe mental illness. She related a scary childhood memory of an elderly aunt who talked incoherent nonsense during a psychotic breakdown.

Nonsense is sometimes a manifestation of mental illness. Chapter 4 will survey the role of nonsense in the life of the mind, including various psychological abnormalities. Even so, on balance, it seems that nonsense is more closely affiliated with mental health than it is with mental illness.

Most people erroneously associate nonsense with repugnance, nothingness, and falsehood, and some associate nonsense with madness. Therefore, they assume that nonsense is inherently unknowable, irrational, unfathomable, and beyond logic and reason. In other words, they think that nonsense presents an impenetrable barrier to rational thought.

A rational study of nonsense sounds like a contradiction in terms. How could there be rational knowledge about something that is meaningless and unintelligible? Discovering that an idea is unintelligible nonsense is supposedly a dead end, insofar as rational inquiry is concerned. Nothing more can or should be investigated by rational means if an idea is found to be meaningless, unintelligible, and nonsensical. As H. H. Price said, "There cannot be evidence for something which is completely unintelligible to us."

A swirl of misconceptions, mistakes, faulty assumptions, and half-truths surrounds the important concept of nonsense. Those errors are so pervasive that people regard them as common sense. Hence, because of that, those ingrained misconceptions about nonsense constitute a hidden, collective cognitive impairment. Unexamined misconceptions about nonsense can sometimes throw off the mind, even when someone is trying hard to think logically, and that is especially so in certain frontier areas of rational inquiry. For instance, we will see later that common misconceptions about nonsense create a formidable obstacle to the rational understanding of life's spiritual dimension.

> Let us, then, give Nonsense its place among the divisions of Humor, and though we cannot reduce it to an exact science, let us acknowledge it as a fine art.
> —*Carolyn Wells*[7]

> It takes a heap of sense to write good nonsense.
> —*Mark Twain*[8]

Nonsense is a creative faculty of certain writers and artists. Normally, it goes without saying that authors want to make sense and convey a meaning to readers' minds. That writers try to say something that is intelligible and meaningful ordinarily is so obvious that there is no reason even to state it. Therefore, writing nonsense deliberately is an art that goes against the grain; it deviates from the norm.

The writings of authors who specialized in the genre of nonsense writing are a logical place to find examples of avowed nonsense. To begin, we will consider five authors who are famous for their nonsense books, and then introduce other authors in subsequent chapters. At this point it would

7   Wells, *A Nonsense Anthology*, xxxiii.

8   Twain, *Mark Twain's Notebooks & Journals*, 303.

be nice to describe some striking characteristic or personality trait that these nonsense writers had in common. Unfortunately, there was no such common characteristic, other than that they were all males who wrote nonsense and that all of them were humorists.

· · · · ·

John Taylor (1578–1653) ferried passengers on the Thames and also wrote volumes of nonsense poetry that he published and sold himself. Taylor, known as "The Water Poet," was a showman and promoter of public spectacles. He once transported a huge man with a prodigious appetite from Kent to London. There, Taylor put the man on display as "The Great Eater of Kent" and charged admission to audiences who flocked to see him.

John Taylor said that "Nonsense is Rebellion."[9] Taylor had little formal education, but he was an intelligent man who saw through intellectual pretense. He realized that nonsense could be used to create an illusion of profundity and scholarship. He wrote:

> Yet I with nonsense could contingerate,
> With catophiscoes terragrophicate,
> And make my selfe admir'd immediately
> By such as understand no more then I.[10]

---

9   Nel, *Dr. Seuss*, 38.

10   Shipley, *Dictionary of Early English*, 173.

Taylor made up meaningless nonsense words for that particular verse. "Contingerate," "catophiscoes" and "terragrophicate" are invented nonsense words that sound like those that professors or doctors might use. In other nonsense verses, Taylor used only meaningful words put together into unintelligible sentences. Here is a sample:

> Oh that my Lungs could bleat like butter'd pease;
> But bleating of my lungs hath caught the itch,
> And are as mangy as the Irish Seas,
> That doth ingender windmills on a Bitch.

> I grant that Rainbowes being lull'd asleep,
> Snort like a woodknife in a Ladies eyes;
> Which maks her grieve to see a pudding creep
> For creeping puddings only please the wise.[11]

* * * *

Edward Lear (1812–1888) was a genial English eccentric who gained fame for his nonsense books for children. Lear's books are selections of nonsense stories, poems, and songs. Lear was a traveling landscape artist, and he illustrated his own books with cartoons and drawings.

Lear made up funny-sounding, meaningless words like "ombliferous," "borascible," "mumbian," "scroobious" and "meloobius" for his nonsense poems. Lear also often put nonsense words into otherwise intelligible letters that he wrote to his friends. Writing from Rome, for instance, he complained to a friend that

---

11 Keegan, *The Penguin Book of English Verse*, 322.

a vile beastly rottenheaded foolbegotten pernicious priggish screaming, tearing, roaring, perplexing, split-mecrackle, crachimecriggle insane ass of a woman is practicing howling below-stairs with a brute of a singing master so horribly, that my head is nearly off![12]

Lear once wrote nonsense that was formatted to look like a letter. He mailed the letter to his friend Evelyn Baring as a joke. Lear wrote:

Thrippsy pillivinx,

Inky tinky pobblebockle abblesquabs?—Flosky!
Beebul trimble flosky!—Okul scratchabibblebongibo,
viddle squibble tog-a-tog, ferrymoyassity amsky
flamsky ramsky damsky crocklefether squiggs.

Flinkywisty pomm,
Slushypipp[13]

. . . .

Charles Dodgson (1832–1889) taught logic and mathematics at Oxford. Dodgson was shy, but as his alter ego, Lewis Carroll, he was the renowned author of *Alice's Adventures in Wonderland* and *Through the Looking-Glass, and What Alice Found There*. Both books combine multiple forms of nonsense to bring strange, alternate worlds alive in readers' minds. In fact, the books reflect two common English phrases that have to do with nonsense, for both "went down the rabbit hole" and

---

12   Lear, *The Complete Nonsense of Edward Lear*, xxi.

13   Lear, *Queery Leary Nonsense*, 6.

"stepped through the looking-glass" denote the experience of finding oneself in nonsensical circumstances.

Much of Carroll's nonsense is based on tricks of logic and plays on words. Carroll also incorporated ideas about certain alternate states of consciousness into his nonsense works. For instance, the Alice books feature dreams, mirror visions, and, possibly, perceptual distortions associated with hallucinogenic mushrooms. Carroll was very interested in paranormal phenomena, too.

Carroll's "Jabberwocky" is perhaps the best-known literary nonsense poem in English. Legions of admirers know the poem by heart, and the meaningless words he invented for the poem have become famous in their own right. The poem begins and ends with this verse:

> 'Twas brillig, and the slithy toves
> Did gyre and gimble in the wabe:
> All mimsy were the borogoves,
> And the mome raths outgrabe.[14]

"Jabberwocky" spawned throngs of earnest interpreters with contending theories about supposed hidden meanings of the poem. The Lewis Carroll Society, dedicated to the study of Carroll and his works, has been active continuously since 1969. Paradoxically, then, "Jabberwocky" is no longer a good example of nonsense to use in formulating a sound theory of meaningless, unintelligible language. "Jabberwocky" carries

---

14   Carroll, *Through the Looking-Glass*, 31.

too much baggage in the form of clashing interpretations and controversial theories. For that reason, we will leave "Jabberwocky" aside and instead consider some of Carroll's other nonsense. Specifically, he wrote fascinating nonsense based on pronouns, conjunctions, figures of speech, and abstract ideas, such as time.

Carroll wrote some lengthy nonsense modeled on complex procedures, such as trials. The final two chapters of *Alice in Wonderland* recount an entire nonsensical trial. The king, serving as judge, begins the trial by ordering the herald to read the accusation. Then the king immediately orders the jury to consider their verdict. The main evidence presented consists of six stanzas of unintelligible nonsense verses such as:

> I gave her one, they gave him two,
> You gave us three or more;
> They all returned from him to you,
> Though they were mine before.[15]

Then, at the end of the trial, the queen demands, "Sentence first—verdict afterward." The trial is made up of nonsensical versions of actual elements of court procedure, yet the many individual unintelligible bits nevertheless combine to create a vivid, coherent mental experience of a strange trial.

---

15   Carroll, *Alice's Adventures in Wonderland*, 183.

· · · ·

Christian Morgenstern (1871–1914) was a gifted German poet whose life was cut short by World War I. Morgenstern had a special talent for humorous, whimsical nonsense poetry with a surrealistic bent. In 1969, on my first visit to Germany, I asked many of the people I met about Christian Morgenstern. Incredibly, practically everyone could recite his most famous poem, "Distinterment."

> Once there was a picket fence
> of interstitial excellence.
>
> An architect much liked its look;—
> protected by the dark he took
>
> the interspaces from the slats
> and built a set of modern flats.
>
> The fence looked nothing as it should,
> since nothing twixt its pickets stood,
>
> This artefact soon fated it,
> the senate confiscated it,
>
> and marked the architect to go
> to Arctic—or Antarctico.[16]

The nonsense poem above was translated from Morgenstern's original German, yet it tells the same meaningless, unintelligible story. Upon reflection, though, the idea of translating nonsense poems from one language into another

---

16 Morgenstern, "Disinternment," 4.

language may seem paradoxical. Translation, supposedly, is creating a new text in one language that has the same meaning as an original text in another language. However, nonsense is meaningless, or devoid of meaning. How, then, could nonsense be translated?

We can accept the paradox, though. In fact, some kinds of nonsense can be translated from one language into other languages, while other kinds of nonsense cannot be translated. Some nonsense does not even need to be translated because it looks the same to people who speak any language. The following nonsense poem by Morgenstern is an illuminating example:

> Laloo Laloo Laloo Laloola
> Kroklokwoffzie? Seemimeemi?
> Siyokronto-pruflipio:
> Biftsi baftsi; hulaleemi:
> quasti basti bo.
> Laloo laloo laloo laloola!
>
> Hontarooroo miromenty
> zaskoo zes roo roo?
> Entypenty, liyolenty
> cleckwapuffsie lue?
> Laloo laloo laloo laloola![17]

---

17 From *Christian Morgenstern: Lullabies, Lyrics and Gallows Songs*.

. . . .

Theodore Geisel (1904–1991) is better known as Dr. Seuss. Dr. Seuss wrote children's books of nonsense poems and stories, which he illustrated with cartoon drawings. Americans tend to identify Dr. Seuss with children's nonsense literature. He was a popular public figure during his lifetime and was honored posthumously on a United States postage stamp. His cartoon characters Horton the Elephant and the Cat in the Hat are recognized, popular symbols or icons of nonsense for children.

Dr. Seuss had an offbeat sense of humor, and he liked to make nonsensical remarks. He once told a group of children that he was trying to invent a boomerang that would not come back. On his deathbed, he looked up at his wife, smiled, and asked, "Am I dead yet?"

In his *Sleep Book*, Dr. Seuss invented a nonsensical sport—sleep talking. In sports, players try to win, and that implies that they are participating consciously. In contrast, people who talk in their sleep are not conscious, and their speech is involuntary. Sleep talking is a sport in Dr. Seuss's nonsense world, though. The world champions are two brothers, Jo and Mo Redd-Zoff, who for fifty-five years have spent their nights "talking their heads off." In that time, the brothers have "talked about laws and they've talked about gauze. They've talked about paws and they've talked about flaws. They've talked quite a lot about old Santa Claus."

Dr. Seuss's list of things the brothers talked about in their sleep consists of unintelligible pairings of unrelated objects joined by the conjunction "and." The incoherence of the list reflects the incoherence of the idea of making a sport of talking in one's sleep. In subsequent contexts, we will find other examples of nonsense that use conjunctions unintelligibly.

Dr. Seuss created plenty of other kinds of nonsense, too, including surprisingly nonsensical curses. Some authorities maintained that curses are inherently meaningless. Apropos, Thomas Hobbes said that "Cursing, Swearing, Reviling, and the like, do not signify as Speech, but as the actions of a tongue accustomed."[18] Daniel Defoe stated that swearing "makes a man's Conversation *unpleasant*, his Discourse *fruitless*, and his Language *Nonsense*."[19] Similarly, H. W. Fowler observed that "When we say *damn*, it relieves us because it is a strong word & yet means nothing."[20]

Since curses are meaningless in the first place, then how could anybody create a nonsensical version of a curse? In the abstract, it doesn't seem conceivable, yet Dr. Seuss created nonsense curses in his comic strip *Hejji* (1935). Hejji was a boy who lived in a mountainous, seemingly Middle Eastern kingdom ruled by the Mighty One. Hejji and the Mighty One

---

18   Hobbes, *Leviathan*, 129.

19   Clark, *Daniel Defoe*, 24.

20   Fowler, *A Dictionary of Modern English Usage*, 681.

uttered colorful, nonsensical swear words that unintelligibly mixed words for body parts with names of astronomical objects. They would swear, for example, "by the wrist of the sun," "by the thumbs of the comet," and "by the tonsils of the Great North Star."

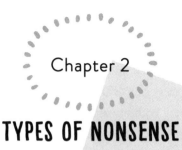

Chapter 2

TYPES OF NONSENSE

*The continual discovery of fresh types
of nonsense, unsystematic though
their classification and mysterious
though their explanation is too
often allowed to remain, has done
on the whole nothing but good.*

J. L. Austin

There are numerous distinct, different types of nonsense. To begin the inquiry, we will consider three patterns or types that clearly emerge in both voluntary and involuntary nonsense. In the process, we will discuss distinctive structural characteristics and assign a name to each type, for there is not a standard system for categorizing, describing, and naming varieties of nonsense. A system of typology—a list of types—is necessary for a rational study of any subject.

Accordingly, this chapter will develop such a system. Then, later, that system will help us comprehend the many strange sights we will see on our journey through the hidden world of nonsense.

Throughout this chapter you will have opportunities to practice some exercises. Students completed these exercises in my university courses and seminars on nonsense. The objectives of the exercises are to activate hidden cognitive faculties of the mind, increase critical thinking abilities, and inspire creative expression.

Categorical Nonsense

Categorical nonsense consists of sentences that are sound in their grammatical structure. Nouns, verbs, adjectives, adverbs, prepositions, and conjunctions are in their correct grammatical positions in relation to each other. Furthermore, sentences of categorical nonsense consist entirely of meaningful words that anyone could look up in a dictionary.

Nonetheless, categorical nonsense is meaningless and unintelligible, and it doesn't convey coherent thoughts to the mind. The meaningful words within the sentence do not fit together meaningfully, despite being in correct grammatical order. Within a sentence of categorical nonsense, the component words are somehow incommensurable or discordant, and they fail to make sense in that particular arrangement.

Categorical nonsense is meaningless and unintelligible because it mismatches subjects and predicates, or things and attributes. That is, categorical nonsense ascribes properties to a thing that are not compatible with a thing of that kind. For example, consider the sentence, "A smiling square root repeated as one necklace an electric limp of potatoes."

Now, a square root is a number, and it can be positive or negative, odd or even, large or small. However, there is no intelligible sense in which a square root could be said to be smiling. Similarly, to talk about a sleeping square root, singing square root, mournful square root, or mauve square root would also be to talk categorical nonsense.

Now consider the sentence, "A scholarly hiccough musically baked numerical stares in a gnawing circle." A hiccough, as a bodily reflex, can be loud or barely audible, distracting or annoying, a normal occurrence, or a sign of a serious illness. However, it makes no sense to say that a hiccough is scholarly. Only a human being can be scholarly, not a hiccough. In other words, the combination "scholarly hiccough" is unintelligible, meaningless categorical nonsense.

Similarly, other words that are paired in the sentence make no sense in combination. The adverb "musically" doesn't fit the verb "baked." The adjective "numerical" does not fit together conceptually with the noun "stares," and "gnawing" and "circle" do not convey an intelligible meaning as combined in that sentence.

In sum, sentences of categorical nonsense fit together grammatically, but not conceptually. I dub this type "categorical nonsense" because it works by transgressing what philosophers know as categories. In philosophical usage, categories are the most basic kinds of things that exist. The theory of categories is complex. Furthermore, mismatches between things and attributes in categorical nonsense need to be explained on a case–by-case basis. Still, it is usually easy to see that categorical nonsense is meaningless and unintelligible.

EXERCISE

Categorical Nonsense

Holiness purses the vestigial lipstick of spontaneity.

A smiling square root sang an electric rainbow.

1. Write an original example of a categorical nonsense sentence.

2. Introspect and record your feelings about this type of nonsense.

Self-Contradictions

Self-contradictions are meaningless and unintelligible because they take back what they say in the very act of saying it. They are grammatically correct sentences that contain only words that are meaningful individually, yet end up meaning nothing because they cancel themselves out.

Contradicting oneself is comparable to taking a step forward only to end up back at the starting point. The net motion forward is zero. Similarly, in a self-contradiction, the net meaning is zero. This type of nonsense is present when C. G. Lichtenberg says, "I thank God that he lets me be an atheist."

To philosophers and logicians, self-contradictions are a primary or quintessential type of nonsense, for the logic that ancient Greek philosophers devised is geared to true-or-false statements of literal meaning. Self-contradictions defeat the purpose of making a statement, however, and end up saying nothing at all because they take themselves back.

Self-contradictions resemble intelligible statements in their grammatical structure, though. Grammatically, "I am naked under my clothes" looks like "I am sweating under my clothes," yet the self-contradiction negates itself and says nothing, while the other is a meaningful statement. In other words, despite their correct grammar, self-contradictions are not a workable formula for making intelligible statements.

C. I. Lewis (1883–1964), an eminent logician, made an astonishing discovery about self-contradictions. Specifically, Lewis proved that any conclusion whatsoever would follow logically from a self-contradiction. His proof is a transparently valid, deductive argument of only four simple, logical steps. Fully understanding the proof requires some background knowledge of formal logic. Still, the implications of the proof can be simply stated.

Suppose, for instance, that we begin with the self-contradictory premise that "a bachelor has been married to a young spinster for twenty years." Then, we could prove any conclusion we might desire in a few indisputably valid steps of logic from that self-contradictory premise. We could prove that purple kangaroos live on Mars or that only 58 people live in Washington, DC, or whatever else we might choose.

Therefore, accepting self-contradictions would bring down the entire structure of rational knowledge by destroying the distinction between truth and falsehood. The law of non-contradiction is one of the three fundamental laws of logical thought propounded by Aristotle. Accepting self-contradictions would abolish reason and all the knowledge that has been built by following the principles of logical reasoning.

Another way of putting Lewis's argument might be to say that a self-contradiction opens up infinite possibilities. Perhaps that is why a bold self-contradiction can make an effective beginning for a book. A self-contradiction attracts readers' interest and attention. The opening line of Dickens's

A Tale of Two Cities is a prime example: "It was the best of times, it was the worst of times." A self-contradiction like that can prepare readers' minds to accept anything and everything that might follow.

EXERCISE

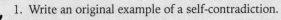

Self-Contradictions

That cannibal you men just ate was the last one in this county.

I'm not an actor, but I play one in the movies.

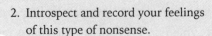

1. Write an original example of a self-contradiction.

2. Introspect and record your feelings of this type of nonsense.

Near English

Near-English nonsense is defined by three characteristics. First, near-English consists of sentences that conform to the grammatical rules of English. Second, the sentences contain, along with ordinary English words, a smattering of made-up, meaningless words. Third, the meaningless words nonetheless sound like English words, not like French words, German words, Italian words, or Spanish words, for meaningless near-English nonsense words are concocted using the phonetic principles of word formation in English.

Consider this declarative sentence: "A shining flamooma quickly turbled and then easily smibbled the five sarbic glusters away." The sentence structure is sound according to the rules of English grammar. Hence, we can deduce from the sentence structure which parts of speech the concocted nonsense words are. Specifically, "flamooma" and "glusters" are nouns, "turbled" and "smibbled" are verbs, and "sarbic" is an adjective.

Now, we could apply the same rules of formulation that define near-English *mutatis mutandis* to, for instance, French. That is, we could start with the correct French grammatical format for declarative sentences. Next, we could put in some ordinary meaningful French words in their correct grammatical positions. Then, we could add a smattering of made-up nonsense words that, because of their phonetic structure, sound like French words. Those steps would produce near-French nonsense.

We could also apply those rules of formulation *mutatis mutandis* to other languages, such as German, Spanish, and Italian. In that way, we would create near-German nonsense, near-Spanish nonsense, and near-Italian nonsense. Therefore, the potential for this type of nonsense exists in practically any language.

Each individual writer's near-English nonsense words sound and look a little different from those of other individuals; we could say that each individual nonsense writer has a distinctive style of writing near-English. Each writer's style leaves a unique imprint on that writer's near-English nonsense words. For example, consider the following near-English nonsense poem by Ogden Nash:

> The sharrot scudders nights in the quastron now,
> The dorlim slinks undeceded in the grost.
> Appetency lights the corb of the guzzard now,
> The ancient beveldric is otley lost.[21]

In my university courses on nonsense, students were able to recognize individual writers' distinctive styles of writing near-English nonsense. In one exercise, students looked at three lists of near-English nonsense words written, respectively, by Edward Lear, Lewis Carroll, and Ogden Nash, and then they looked at several near-English nonsense words without knowing which author wrote them. Most students were able to easily identify which near-English nonsense word was written by which particular author.

---

21 Nash, "Geddondillo," 23.

ExERciSE

Distinctive Styles of Writing Near-English Nonsense

A simplified version of the original exercise is reproduced below.

EDWARD LEAR	LEWIS CARROLL	OGDEN NASH
scroobius	brillig	quastron
meloobius	galumphinx	undeceded
ombliferous	wabe	grost
borascible	mimsy	corb
slobaciously	borogores	guzzard
himmeltanious	frabjous	beveldric
pomskillious	uffish	treduty

Now look at the three near-English nonsense words below.
Which word belongs with which author?

1. slithy

2. dorlim

3. crumboblious

The majority of students correctly matched "slithy" to Lewis
Carroll, "dorlim" to Ogden Nash, and "crumboblious" to
Edward Lear. Distinctiveness of style in writing near-English
does not pertain solely to professional nonsense writers, either.
In written exercises, my students created their own original
examples of most types of nonsense we studied. In one exercise,
students wrote original near-English nonsense sentences.

When I compared hundreds of students' written exercises, it was apparent that an individual's style of near-English was recognizable, for the various non-English words that the individual created all resembled each other. In other words, a person's style of near-English is a sort of fingerprint, somehow reflecting that individual's mind. As we move forward, additional, similar connections between nonsense and the mind will emerge.

EXERCISE

Near-English

A shining flazoma easily turbled five sarbic muffards away.

Some lazy ink trunes spoogled dardly on the green lummuck.

1. Write an original example of a near-English sentence.

2. Introspect, then record your feelings and impressions about this type of nonsense.

· · · ·

The three types that we analyzed up to this point are only a small fraction of the types of nonsense that occur. I found more than seventy types in my own four-and-a-half-decade study of the subject. However, a list of seventy-plus types would be too long for any practical purpose and too difficult to learn or remember.

A system of classification that takes three different levels of nonsense into account is simpler and more comprehensible. First we will consider the structural principle that all types of nonsense have in common. Second, we will discuss how different types of nonsense can be combined. Then, third, we will see how a corresponding type of nonsense can be built around practically any structure of ordinary language.

Nonsense of each type follows some rules and breaks others in its own distinctive combination. The three types of nonsense that we discussed above follow the grammatical rules that govern ordinary sentence structure. That is, categorical nonsense, self-contradictions, and near-English conform to standard grammatical rules for sentences.

Each of these three types of nonsense also breaks some other standard rules and conventions of ordinary language. Hence, categorical nonsense violates the rules and regulations as to which properties belong with which things. A number, for instance, can be large or small, positive or negative, cardinal or ordinal, but it cannot be lazy, intelligent, or self-indulgent, and that makes sentences like "A self-indulgent, lazy 19 greeted an intelligent 7" categorical nonsense.

Self-contradictions violate the basic rules that define making a meaningful statement. A statement says something that is true or false, while a self-contradiction takes itself back and says nothing at all.

In addition to obeying standard grammatical rules of sentence formation, near-English also follows standard phonetic rules of forming English words. However, near-English violates the fundamental rule or convention that when we speak, we use only actual meaningful words with standard dictionary definitions. In sum, categorical nonsense, self-contradictions, and near-English follow some rules of language and break other rules of language, each in a distinctive combination.

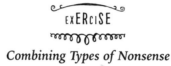

ExERciSE

Combining Types of Nonsense

The moping shoes of logic silently screamed chibbled nanks of colorless blue rainbow food.

Droonly dreaming bread electrically chastled a married bachelor.

1. Write an original sentence combining near-English, categorical nonsense, and self-contradiction.

2. Introspect, then record your feelings and impressions of writing this sentence.

All types of nonsense reflect this same underlying structural formula of following some rules and breaking others in a distinctive and unintelligible combination. That is the universal structural principle of nonsense of all types and the center and circumference of the concept of nonsense itself. In effect, this universal structural principle is what nonsense is—the essence of nonsense. Using this structural principle, we can characterize each distinct type of nonsense by specifying which rules of language it follows and which rules of language it breaks. Each type of nonsense, then, can be designed as a unique and distinctive combination of rule-following and rule-breaking.

Nonsense and Cartoons

Cartooning, too, follows some rules and breaks other rules to create powerful aesthetic and psychological effects. That is, cartoonists follow some rules of realistic drawing and break other rules of realistic drawing to entertain, amuse, inform, and inspire their readers. Nonsense is structurally akin to cartoons, and that reminds us of the affinity mentioned earlier between nonsense writing and cartooning.

Edward Lear, Dr. Seuss, and Shel Silverstein, for example, drew cartoons to illustrate their books of nonsense poetry for children. To say the least, then, it is interesting that these same artists would be talented in two different forms of following rules and breaking rules. At least two familiar types of nonsense occur only in cartoons or in graphic form: mock writing and nonsense letters.

Mock Writing

Mock writing is a pictorial form of nonsense often found in cartoons. Mock writing consists of predominantly meaningless, unintelligible marks like squiggles, scrawling, doodles, or sometimes just parallel straight lines. The meaningless marks look like writing that is somewhat out of focus or too far away to be seen clearly enough to read. Mock writing resembles writing, but it conveys no meaningful content or message.

The purpose of mock writing in cartoons is to create an illusion or impression of writing. Sometimes cartoonists draw in a few actual letters among the meaningless marks to enhance the illusion. Also, the placement of the meaningless marks in the cartoon shows us they are supposed to represent writing. Cartoonists inscribe mock writing on some other figure in the drawing—a flip chart or a poster on a wall or lamppost. The convention signals that something is supposedly written there, but we are not to try to decipher it. The meaning does not matter because there is no meaning.

Smudgy equations and mathematical symbols scrawled on a blackboard are another familiar form of mock writing. To most people, they epitomize the incomprehensibility of modern science. In fact, they are probably the best-known cartoon icon of unintelligibility.

Nonsense Letters

Nonsense letters are meaningless, unintelligible marks that imitate the general appearance of alphabetic letters.

However, they do not belong to any actual, existing alphabet. The person who invents such marks has actual letters in mind as a sort of model. Still, nonsense letters are not exact replicas of actual letters.

Some children with developmental disabilities draw nonsense letters. When they are asked to draw letters of the alphabet, they draw meaningless marks that resemble letters instead. This shows that they have a vague idea of what letters look like but are unable to copy them.

Dr. Seuss made up an entire nonsense alphabet of meaningless letters, such as "yuzz." In *On Beyond Zebra* he explained, "There are things beyond Z that most people don't know." He needed extra letters because:

> In the places I go there are things that I see
> That I never could spell if I stopped with the Z.
> I'm telling you this cause you're one of my friends.
> My alphabet starts where your alphabet ends.

Dr. Seuss's purpose was humor. However, people have created nonsense letters and nonsense alphabets for fraud, hoaxes, or imposture, using concocted nonsense letters to create meaningless, unintelligible inscriptions on stones. Fake alphabets have been used to create manuscripts, with the resulting inscriptions or manuscripts looking like they were written in some exotic, unknown alphabet. Hoaxers' productions sometimes kept archaeologists or linguists busy for years trying to decipher nonsense.

Integrating Nonsense

Here we will investigate cases of combining multiple types of nonsense into a more complex unit.

Nonsense of several types can be combined into one structure. This section will draw examples from multiple types of nonsense from Lewis Carroll's classic Alice books that Carroll wove into a unified work of literature. Similarly, as we shall see, other nonsense writers also commonly put a variety of types together into a single poem or story.

Apparently, though, readers almost never realize that such a work is composed of more than one distinct type of nonsense. That is what I observed in my courses on nonsense. People seem to have an undifferentiated experience even when several distinct types of nonsense are used in a poem.

The same students immediately realized that there were different types of nonsense in the poems once I pointed it out to them. Then it seemed so obvious to them that they wondered why they did not notice it before. Several types of nonsense can be combined in a single grammatical sentence. Consider the sentences below:

> The moping shoes of logic silently screamed chibbled nanks of colorless blue rainbow food.

> Droonly dreaming bread electrically chastled a married bachelor.

The sentences are fairly short grammatically correct declaratives, yet each sentence uses three different types of nonsense—categorical nonsense, self-contradiction, and near-English. Therefore, diverse types of nonsense can be integrated, even on a small scale, to function as a unit.

Nonsense of a corresponding type can be modeled on any structure of ordinary language, and nonsense occurs at every organizational level of language. There are levels of language: phonemes, syllables, words, sentences, recipes, stories, essays, plays, novels, scientific texts. Then, additionally, there are special compartments of language reserved for medicine, the law, science, and their brands of professional jargon. The complexity ranges up to the level of entire languages—French, Italian, Greek, English, and all the others. Each and every one of those elements, levels, compartments, and languages can potentially serve as a format for creating a corresponding type of nonsense.

Thus far, we have looked at three types of nonsense at the level of sentences: categorical nonsense, self-contradictions and near-English. Later, we will come back and consider some additional types of nonsense that occur primarily in sentence form. Meanwhile, this section will examine a bonanza of new types that are inherent in the multilevel structure of nonsense. We will begin with the smallest type of nonsense that exists.

Nonsense Syllables

bez	bup	dax	fip	gan	haj
jad	jeg	mof	pog	sab	nud

A nonsense syllable is a meaningless, unintelligible combination of letters formed by putting a vowel between two consonants. A nonsense syllable must not form an actual word or standard abbreviation. Hence, "cab," "can," and "cap" are not nonsense syllables since they are actual words. "Feb" and "aug" are not nonsense syllables since they are standard abbreviations for months of the year.

Nonsense syllables are perhaps the smallest quanta of meaningless language that exists. They are an important type of nonsense for scientific inquiry. For example, psychologists use nonsense syllables in experiments on learning and memory. Also, communications technicians use certain nonsense syllables known as "logatoms" to test telephone circuitry.

Nonsense syllables take the place of words in scat singing and doo-wop music. Scat singing is a form of jazz in which singers substitute improvised, meaningless verbiage for words of songs. Louis Armstrong, Ella Fitzgerald, and Al Jarreau are noted for scat singing. These great artists sing songs that in whole or in part consist of nonsense syllables instead of words.

Ella Fitzgerald's song "Flying Home" consists solely of nonsense syllables. Still, some who listened to the song in my courses said they could make out meaningful words occasionally. The students enjoyed this exercise because they discovered that no two listeners ever heard the same words in the song, and they realized that the supposed words came from their imagination.

ExERcISE

Nonsense Syllables

jad
jeg
pog
sab
nud

1. Write some nonsense syllables.

2. Introspect, then record your feelings and impressions about the mental process of writing nonsense syllables.

Nonsense Names

Proper names are words that denote individual persons or places; for example, "Henry," "Jane," and "Paris." Some think of proper names as the simplest kind of word that exists. After all, there seems to be a transparent, one-to-one relationship between a proper name and the person or thing it denotes. Besides, proper names are an indispensable fixture of everyday conversation. Thus, we use a man's proper name to refer to him, address him, summon him, identify him in a photograph, or, originally, to christen him. Constant usage makes us feel we understand proper names perfectly.

American society allows a lot of latitude in bestowing names on people. I could concoct original, crazy-sounding names: "Abezagaffa," "Mazzakakka," and "Elvisimadonna." Then I could legally bestow them on my infant children. Thereafter, these strange words would be the legal names of my children. They would not be nonsense names but actual proper names registered on birth certificates.

We can create nonsensical proper names in at least two ways, however. First, we can invent capitalized nonsense words like "Maybotrene," "Adaluncatif," and "Torbunkle." Then, without ever bestowing them on anyone, we can drop them into isolated sentences as follows:

> Maybotrene is never here.

> The sect of the son of Adaluncatif will prevail.

> Torbunkle is not in trouble.

Such sentences do not provide enough contextual information to make clear who Maybotrene, Adaluncatif, or Torbunkle might be. Invented capitalized words are not meaningful proper names unless we flesh out characters to bear them. Instead, these bizarre, unintelligible words constitute nonsense names.

Still, they *look* like proper names, for they are capitalized and they occupy the same grammatical positions in sentences that meaningful proper names do. Moreover, the conventions that govern proper names are deeply ingrained in our minds from constant usage. Hence, despite being meaningless, nonsense names induce a weird, indecipherable sense of a person or entity. Something strange happens when we read sentences like "The sect of Adaluncatif will prevail." We experience a vague idea of an indeterminate personage or being that somehow corresponds to "Adaluncatif." Later, we shall see that this phenomenon is of considerable historical significance.

We can also create nonsense names by capitalizing abstract nouns and then positioning them grammatically like proper names. Lewis Carroll used this technique in both his Alice books. The passages below are prime examples:

> Alice sighed wearily. "I think you might do something better with the time," she said, "than wasting it in asking riddles that have no answers."
>
> "If you knew Time as well as I do," said the Hatter, "you wouldn't talk about wasting IT. It's HIM."
>
> "I don't know what you mean," said Alice.

"Of course you don't!" the Hatter said, tossing his head contemptuously.

"I dare say you never even spoke to Time!"

"Perhaps not," Alice cautiously replied, "but I know I have to beat time when I learn music."

"Ah! That accounts for it," said the Hatter. "He won't stand beating. Now if you only kept on good terms with him, he'd do almost anything you liked with the clock. For instance, suppose it were nine o'clock in the morning, just time to begin lessons: you'd only have to whisper a hint to Time, and around goes the clock in the twinkling! Half-past one, time for dinner!"[22]

"I see nobody on the road," said Alice.

"I only wish I had such eyes," the King remarked in a fretful tone. "To be able to see Nobody! And at that distance too! Why it's as much as I can do to see real people, by this light!"[23]

As nonsense writing, it is funny. However, various philosophers took this odd way of talking seriously. They apparently assumed that all words get their meanings by being names of things. This assumption was the root cause of much nonsense in the form of meaningless philosophical speculation. For example, the philosopher Heidegger wrote as though the word "nothing" were a proper name. He said, "Nothing nothings itself." The sentence is nonsensical, but Heidegger and his disciples thought it expressed a profound truth.

22 Carroll, *Alice's Adventures in Wonderland*, 101–102.

23 Carroll, *Through the Looking-Glass*, 136.

Nonsense Dates

Orientation to time is an essential cognitive faculty. To function in modern society, we need to know which day, month, and year it is. The names of the days of the week and months of the year are a vital part of language. We begin to comprehend this system of terminology at about five or six years of age. Then, thereafter, we use it practically every day for the rest of our lives.

It is possible to create nonsense that sounds like these familiar words. For example, "Septober the eighth" and "Fumbleday the twentieth of Juluary" sound like dates. We can even make up sentences like "Magoona the Great died in late Februember, 284 B.D."

The ordinary terminology of days, weeks, months, and years is indelibly imprinted in our minds, so a nonsense phrase or sentence like the above example produces a vague sense of an indeterminate date.

Dr. Seuss's hilarious book *October the First* utilizes these principles. The book promises kids they can have anything and everything they want when Octember the first rolls around. We do not have to go that far to create a nonsense date. "June the ninety-third" and "the sixty-first day of December" do not make sense, either.

. . . .

We went from nonsense syllables to two types of nonsense that can occur as single words, namely, nonsense names and nonsense dates. Next, we consider some types of nonsense that are made by putting multiple different words together. Note that we can do that without necessarily having to create an actual sentence.

Meaningless Word Strings

By eliminating syntax, we can string meaningful words together into unintelligible sequences, then punctuate the resulting incoherent processions of words to look like sentences. Such meaningless, unintelligible word strings are devoid of grammatical order, so they do not convey coherent thoughts to the mind.

Normally, when we speak or write, the mind automatically puts words together into proper grammatical arrangement. Hence, meaningless word strings are a difficult type of nonsense to compose. The process taxes the mind because grammatical order seems to keep inserting itself unbidden. Many of my students reported that writing meaningless word strings was a vexatious, frustrating experience for them, yet they also said that it was interesting and informative. The process made them aware of the complex automatic mental processes that underlie ordinary speech.

ExERcisE

Meaningless Word Strings

Green it thankful swings if how zest.

Money transcendence any explodes hooray category if.

1. Write an original meaningless word string.

b. Introspect, then record your feelings and impressions about the mental process of writing a meaningless word string.

• • • •

Edward Lear, Lewis Carroll, and Dr. Seuss all used types of nonsense that are based on specific parts of speech. First we will look at a type of nonsense that plays tricks with conjunctions; then we will examine a type that uses pronouns unintelligibly.

Conjunctive Nonsense

Conjunctions are words used to connect words, phrases, clauses, or sentences. "And," "or," "but," and "because" are conjunctions.

Normally, context makes it clear how the things joined by a conjunction are supposed to be related. Hence, it is easy to comprehend the sentence "My dog and cat fight every day." Nor would anyone have any trouble comprehending a sentence like "My Uncle Hamperd ate fish and chips and bacon and eggs and bread and butter and had pie and ice cream for dessert."

However, Lear's and Carroll's nonsense verses use conjunctions that have no intelligible relationship to each other. The mind draws a blank when trying to figure out how rainbows and knives or muscles and hives, or hurdles and mumps or poodles and pumps, could possibly be related. Similarly, putting shoes, ships, sealing wax, cabbages, and kings together without providing a unifying context makes no sense. The mind is unable to establish any meaningful linkages among such wildly disparate items such as "forks and hope" and "smiles and soap."[24]

Non-junctive nonsense is unintelligible because it uses conjunctions to put things together that have no business being put together that way. It is a common technique of nonsense writers. In fact, it helps structure the most familiar nonsense verse in English. In the nursery rhyme that follows, no context is provided that enables us to see how the cat and the fiddle are supposed to be connected. Nor can we figure out what the little dog's laughing has to do with the dish and the spoon running away together:

---

24   Carroll, *The Hunting of the Snark*, 22.

Hey diddle diddle
The cat and the fiddle
The cow jumped over the moon.
The little dog laughed to see such sport
And the dish ran away with the spoon.

Nonreferential Pronouns

They told me you had been to her
 And mentioned me to him.
She gave me a good character.
 But said I could not swim.

He sent them word I had not gone,
 (We know it to be true)
If she should push the matter on
 What would become of you?

 …

If I or she should chance to be
 Involved in this affair,
He trusts to you to see them free
 Exactly as we were.

My notion was that you had been
 (Before she had this fit)
An obstacle that came between
 Him, and ourselves, and it.

Don't let him know she liked them best,
 For this must ever be
A secret kept from all the rest,
 Between yourself and me.[25]

---

25 Carroll, *Alice's Adventures in Wonderland*, 183–184.

Nothing whatsoever in the verbal or situational context of Carroll's poem tells us who or what "they," "he," "she," "it," "you," or "I" are supposed to be. Consequently, the sentences, though grammatically correct, run on and on without making a point. A mild confusion or disoriented state sets in, and the reader's mind floats free.

> Uncle Hamperd and Aunt Florene went downtown and bought a dozen doughnuts and they brought the doughnuts home. He ate ten of the doughnuts, she ate one, and they had one left. So, they divided it in half, but he ate both halves.

This story makes sense because the referents of the pronouns are clearly identified. However, Carroll's verses above are nonsense because there is no way of telling what the pronouns supposedly denote. This particular technique of nonsense writing is hard to master. Participants in my courses and workshops experienced little trouble writing near-English nonsense, categorical nonsense, and numerous other types; in fact, they found it interesting and enjoyable. However, they experienced considerable difficulty writing nonreferential pronouns. They described the process as frustrating and mind-numbing.

Numerative Nonsense

Numerative nonsense is meaningless, unintelligible language that is modeled on number terminology. This particular type of nonsense is difficult to classify, for numerative nonsense occurs in several distinct kinds. The same problem also arises with some other types of nonsense, though. Therefore, we need to add another precept to our system of classifications.

Nonsense of one type may occur in multiple distinct subtypes. Numerative nonsense is found in at least four distinct subtypes. First, actual numbers can be put into a context in which there is no possibility of determining what they are supposed to enumerate. The number words just dangle in a void. Lewis Carroll produced interesting examples of this type of nonsense; consider the verse below:

> I gave her one, they gave him two,
> You gave us three or more.[26]

This sentence invites the question of what "one," "two," or "three" is referencing. Nothing in the verbal or situational context enables us to answer that question. So, here, the words "one," "two" and "three" do not enumerate anything.

Similarly, in *Through the Looking-Glass*, the Red Queen invites Alice to a banquet. When she arrives, the guests sing a song, purportedly to greet her. The chorus of the song runs, "And welcome Queen Alice with thirty-times-three," and then, "And welcome Queen Alice with ninety-times-nine."[27] The trouble is nothing enables us to answer the questions "thirty-times-three what?" or "ninety-times-nine what?" And so Alice is left wondering what those numbers are supposed to enumerate.

---

26 Carroll, *Alice's Adventures in Wonderland*, 183.

27 Carroll, *Through the Looking-Glass*, 192–193.

Or, secondly, one can force meaningful number terminology into combinations or arrangements that do not make sense. Examples would be "This is the eleventy-tenth time you've been late this week" or "There is a 185 percent chance of rain tomorrow."

Then, thirdly, one can create meaningless, unintelligible verbiage that looks and sounds like number terminology. For example, "Uncle Hamperd is worth five batrillion, three fazillion, twenty-nine bombastillion dollars and sixteen cents." Carl Barks was a master of this type of nonsense.

Or, fourthly, one can write nonsense in the format of numerical calculations or mathematical equations. For example, Dr. Seuss included an incomprehensible equation in *The Cat in the Hat Songbook*. According to the song "I Can Figure Figures,"

> Twenty thousand turtles times ten tin tops
> Plus fifteen billion buttons
> Minus seven lollipops.
> Divide by two bananas,
> That makes eleventeen
> French fries, noodles and a green string bean.

· · · ·

Next, we will consider two important types of nonsense that are based on specific constructions. For, to this point, the nonsensical sentences that we studied were, for the most part, declarative in their grammatical structure. However, strikingly different effects are created by nonsense in different grammatical formats.

CHAPTER 2

Counterfactual Conditional Nonsense

Understanding the meaning of a sentence that begins with "if," a conditional sentence, is sometimes tricky. This is especially so in the case of counterfactual conditionals, for the first clause of a counterfactual conditional statement expresses something contrary to the fact; for example, "If I had known." Counterfactual conditions puzzle philosophers because it is difficult to explain how such statements could be meaningful or intelligible. Therefore, conditional statements of that kind are a particularly good format for creating memorable nonsense. As C. G. Lichtenberg said, "This is certainly one of the strangest combinations of words possible in human language: 'If I had not been born, I would be free of all my troubles.'"

Counterfactual conditionals can be useful for shaping future behavior in light of past experiences. Hence, thinking "If I had a flashlight with me, we could have found our way home" is useful for planning future walks with the family. Counterfactual conditionals are also good for wishful thinking that avoids reality; for example, "If there had been one more number correct on that lottery ticket I bought last month, I would be on vacation in the Caribbean now."

Some counterfactual conditionals have a paradoxical quality that challenges the philosophical mind. Also, counterfactual conditionals can foster whimsical thinking that is enjoyable for its own sake and often used for self-deception. Their puzzling paradoxical quality and their whimsical escapist

66

quality make counterfactual conditionals an excellent format for creating entertaining and mind-stretching nonsense.

Nonsense Questions

Nonsense questions are a serious subject because of their effects on the mind. Nonsense that is grammatically formatted as an interrogative sentence sometimes adversely affects people's thought processes and interferes with their logical reasoning. Accordingly, nonsense questions are particularly important in the search for rational knowledge, so it is not surprising that various great thinkers have weighed in on the topic of meaningless, unintelligible interrogatives. Unsurprisingly, they also expressed a variety of different opinions about how we ought to respond to nonsense questions.

C. S. Lewis (1898–1963), for example, was an eminent twentieth-century religious thinker and writer, and an author of children's classics. He encountered plenty of nonsense questions as he pondered the spiritual dimension of life and observed that they are a pervasive phenomenon of religious thought. Lewis wrote:

> Can a mortal ask questions which God finds unanswerable? Quite easily, I should think. All nonsense questions are unanswerable...Is yellow square or round? Probably half the questions we ask—half our great theological and metaphysical problems—are like that.[28]

---

28   Lewis, *A Grief Observed*, 69.

Aldous Huxley (1894–1963), another modern pioneer of spiritual thought, expressed a similar opinion about non-sense questions. In doing so, he invoked Lewis Carroll's famous nonsense riddle, or riddle with no conventional or adjoined answer: "Why is a raven like a writing desk?"[29] This riddle is part of the Mad Tea Party in Carroll's *Alice in Wonderland*, and, as Carroll said, "The Riddle, as originally invented, had no answer at all."[30] Even so, what the answer might be soon became a popular topic of conversation and speculation, and almost a parlor game. Huxley compared the phenomenon to humankind's philosophical and religious quest:

> To a nonsensical question, one can make almost any answer one likes...It really makes no difference. My own belief is that all the riddles of the Universe, in the form in which philosophical tradition has presented them to us, belong to the why-is-a-raven-like-a-writing-desk category. They are nonsensical riddles, questions asked not about reality but about words. The devils whiled away their time discussing fixed fate, free will, foreknowledge absolute: Job and Dostoevsky rack their brains over the wherefore of human sufferings. But they really might just as well have spent their time and energy over the question: "What is a mouse when it spins?"

The fundamental trouble with all theological and meta-physical speculation is the fact that, in the very process of

---

29   Carroll, *Alice's Adventures in Wonderland*, 97.

30   Ibid., preface (no page number is given).

becoming speculation, it almost inevitably becomes nonsensical.

Nonsense questions are often funny, too. Consider, for example, the following familiar children's riddle: "An airplane crashed exactly on the border between two countries. In which country were the survivors buried?" Figuring out the self-contradiction solves the riddle and makes children laugh.

Dr. Seuss's *The Cat's Quizzer* is a little book of funny, wacky questions, asked just for laughs. Some of them are nonsense: "Are there more A's or Z's in the alphabet?" The book also asks, "There are flashlights for when it's dark. Are there flashdarks for when it is light?"

Nonsense questions are used in intelligence work. This came to light in the 1980s as a result of a successful suit under the Freedom of Information Act. The outcome forced the CIA to release one of their secret interrogation manuals to the public.

In the photocopied pages of the manual that were released, much of the text was blacked out in that familiar CIA manner. What did come through was revealing, though, for it showed that the CIA used nonsense questions for interrogating suspected spies or double agents and breaking them down.

The power of nonsense questions comes from the fact that as children we learn that we are expected to answer when someone asks us a question. This lesson gets reinforced constantly for the rest of our lives. Hence, the interrogative mood lends a compelling quality to nonsense and makes people uneasy. They feel as though they are under an obligation to answer, even though the question makes no sense, so asking people nonsense questions is an effective method of pressuring them.

In effect, a question is part statement and part command. Accordingly, the familiar grammatical distinctions among the following four different types of sentences are oversimplified and cause confusion. For, actually, their distinctions are not as sharp, their definitions are not as accurate, and their functions are not as distinct as is generally believed.

Hence, according to standard grammatical definitions, a declarative sentence makes a statement or describes a state of affairs. An interrogative sentence asks a question. An imperative sentence issues a command or makes a request, and an exclamatory sentence expresses strong emotion.

In reality, however, the different grammatical structures of sentences and their corresponding different functions are mixed up, and they overlap. For example, questions and statements are alike in that they both convey information. Thus, the context or situation supplies some information that establishes the meaning of the question even when someone asks only "Who?" or "Why?" or "When?"

Questions and commands are also alike in that they both direct someone to say or do something in response. When we ask someone a question, for example, we expect an answer. When issuing a command, we expect someone to comply. Accordingly, there is always some residual imperative force in a question, even if it is meaningless and unintelligible. In fact, this helps explain the strange hold nonsense questions have on the mind.

EXERCISE

Nonsense Questions

Does the number nine prefer to bounce or bluster?

How many smufflepuffs can a voodle recite?

1. Write an original nonsense question.

2. Introspect, then record your feelings and the mental process of writing a nonsense question. How did the process differ from writing nonsensical declarative sentences?

Nonsense Definitions

A definition is a statement that tells what a word means. Clear definitions make communication possible. Hence, they are essential for rational inquiry and for the regulation of human societies. They are indispensable tools for science, mathematics, commerce, and law.

> POMSKIZILLIOUS: The coast scenery may truly be called "pomskizillious" and "gromphibberous," being as no words can describe its magnificence.
> —*Edward Lear*

> DEFINITION: God is the shortest distance between zero and infinity. In which direction? one may ask. ± We shall reply that His first name is not Jack, but Plus-and-Minus. And one should say: God is the shortest distance between 0 and ∞ in either direction.
> —*Alfred Jarry*

Nonsense can be formatted to resemble definitions, as the above examples show. Nonsense writers make up these meaningless definitions to be humorous, and readers are then unlikely to mistake the humorous purpose.

Sometimes, though, nonsense definitions create convincing illusions that meaningless words make sense. In these cases they can retard the progress of knowledge or help perpetuate and maintain brutal regimes. Nonsense definitions often have played a leading role in religion, politics, philosophy, and science. In later chapters we will encounter particular examples of this important phenomenon.

Nonsense also can be modeled on language for giving instructions on how to do something or carry out a procedure. Now we will turn to a couple types of nonsense formatted as instructions. And they remind us, again, that a corresponding type of nonsense can be built around virtually any structure of ordinary meaningful language.

Nonsense Directions

Giving directions to someone on how to reach a distant place is a basic social and linguistic skill that is obligatory for almost everyone. Consequently, everyone is familiar with stock phrases used for giving directions, as in these examples: "Turn right on the next corner" or "Go straight on down this road and take a left turn at the third intersection." As a result, people experience these phrases as familiar, even when they are used in a meaningless, unintelligible, nonsensical way.

Peter Pan told Wendy the way to Neverland using the nonsensical direction "Second to the right, and straight on till morning."[31] The words and phrases do sound like directions, yet neither Peter Pan nor the narrator, nor any other information in the novel, provides a context in which those words would make intelligible sense.

Other patterns could also be used for writing nonsense directions. For instance, we could put some meaningless near-English words into sentences along with the stock

---

31 Barrie, *Peter Pan*, 49.

terminology used for giving directions. "Continue south on this highway until you come to a plausamus hossamedge on the left, then turn right at the next intersection" or "To reach a splendid sploafer like you've always dreamed of, walk five miles down this road and then platterate at the next monastrum." Similarly, many other patterns and designs could also be used for writing nonsense directions. In other words, we could create, indefinitely, many distinct subtypes of nonsense directions.

Nonsense Recipes

Unintelligible nonsense can be designed to look like instructions for performing a procedure. In fact, nonsense could be modeled on practically any kind of set of instructions. Nonsense could be tailored to look like instructions for playing games, repairing machines, building airplanes, assembling toys, growing flowers, or performing scientific experiments.

Apparently, though, nonsense recipes are nonsense writers' preferred subtype of meaningless, unintelligible instructions. Edward Lear wrote a mini cookbook of three nonsensical recipes. "To Make An Amblongous Pie" never explains what the main ingredient, amblongouses, are. Similarly, "To Make Crumbobblious Cutlets" offers no clue about how to find "4 gallons of clarified crumbobblious sauce." Some of the directions for making crumbobblious cutlets are self-contradictory, too. The recipe says, "Procure some strips of beef, and having cut them into the smallest possible pieces, proceed to cut them still smaller, eight or nine times." Then, just when the dish is apparently ready to be served, Lear's recipe says to "throw the whole thing out the window."

Dr. Seuss also wrote a nonsense recipe with a meaningless, unintelligible ingredient. The recipe calls for adding "a hunk of something…Hunk of chuck-a-luck, I think."[32] This recipe for Glunker Stew requires a nonsensical cooking utensil, too: "a special frazzle-spade." Finally, the concoction needs to be "spuggled" in a mixer.

Evidently, then, a variety of different ingredients can be used for cooking up nonsense recipes. Or, more generally, nonsense can be laid out to look like a set of instructions for performing procedures of practically any kind. Furthermore, in my course exercises, students wrote nonsensical versions of various kinds of instructions for procedures by following patterns. Students in the courses were also able to write nonsense that imitated the appearance and sound of specialized technical language of various professions.

Mock Professional Jargon

Meaningless, unintelligible verbiage can be tailored to look and sound like the technical terminology of medical doctors, scientists, or attorneys. I wrote the below passage of mock medical nonsense to serve as an example of more professional jargon. This type of nonsense is usually created for comic effect or for the purpose of deception.

---

32   Seuss, *I Can Lick 30 Tigers Today*, no page is given.

If they become infected, splanginating fractures of the posterior mesonuncular bone may cause pongulated mithritis of the overlying blenoid veins. Therefore, physicians treating these injuries need to check frequently for flubosis of the epithymial joint and truncal glabosis.

Dr. Seuss's book *You're Only Old Once* contains humorous mock professional jargon. The book is about an elderly gentleman's visit to a medical clinic for a physical examination. Mock medical nonsense is posted on funny signs in the hallways of the clinic. The signs point the way to Optoglymics, Dermoglymics, and Nooronetics.

Honest John, the fox in Walt Disney's animated film classic *Pinocchio*, spoke mock professional jargon. Honest John posed as a doctor to lure the little puppet into a life of sin on Pleasure Island. He diagnosed Pinocchio with "compound transmission of the pandemonium with percussion and spasmodic fabric disintegration" and "complicated syncopation of the dilla-dilla."[33]

Only experts in relevant technical knowledge can distinguish mock professional jargon from the real thing. For example, are sulfoprotium prioxide, bandekleinic acid, and methylenic-hydrozochloride chemical compounds or nonsense? Only someone well versed in chemistry can tell. This helps explain how impostors pass themselves off as attorneys, doctors, or scientists. Laypersons cannot distinguish impostors' nonsense versions from actual professional terminology.

33 Disney, *Pinocchio*.

ᴇxᴇʀᴄɪSᴇ

Mock Professional Jargon

If they become infected, splanginating fractures of the mesonuncular bone may cause pongulated mithritis of the blenoid veins.

1. Write an original example of mock medical nonsense.

2. Introspect, then record your feelings and impressions about the mental process of writing mock medical jargon.

· · · · ·

To review, we developed a typology that takes three different structural levels of nonsense into account. Namely, we examined the underlying structural principles that all types of nonsense have in common. We analyzed structures that are compounded of multiple distinct types of nonsense, and we showed that nonsense can be modeled on any structure of ordinary language. In the process, an interesting psychological effect related to various types of nonsense has become visible.

Nonsense of each type produces some characteristic effects of the structure upon which it is modeled. Nonsense can be modeled on virtually any structure of language, and when it is, the nonsense, despite being meaningless and unintelligible, re-creates some effects characteristic of that structure. For example, a nonsense name sometimes produces a vague mental sense of a corresponding person or entity bearing the name. A nonsense date can create a sense of an indeterminate day, month, or year. A nonsense definition can create a convincing sense that a meaningless, unintelligible word has a meaning. Nonsense questions can make people strive to find meaningful answers, and mock professional jargon can sometimes persuade a layperson that an impostor is a rocket scientist or a doctor or an attorney.

In other words, nonsense mimics some effects of the form of intelligible language upon which it is modeled. Apparently, then, when there is no meaning, the form of language takes precedence over the content or some properties of particular structures of language transfer onto their corresponding types of nonsense. Discussing the effects of nonsense, or how nonsense affects people, naturally leads us to another form of language, one that produces curious, useful, and pleasant effects.

Figurative Nonsense

Like nonsense, figures of speech serve as the special effects of language. As Aristotle said, "Midway between the unintelligible and the commonplace, it is a metaphor which most produces knowledge." Figures of speech add beauty, color, energy, and emphasis to what is said or written. Metaphor, simile, oxymoron, alliteration, onomatopoeia, personification, irony, and hyperbole, to cite examples, are figures of speech. Experts in literature and rhetoric also know of dozens of other common but lesser-known figures of speech that work "undercover," without being recognized.

Figures of speech stir up feelings. Accordingly, they are common in poetry, fiction, advertising, sermons, political speeches, and other language intended to please, challenge, or persuade people. Figures of speech are also common in everyday conversation, and people use them automatically, without thinking about them.

Nonsense can be modeled on practically any figure of speech. Since there are dozens of figures of speech, that means there are dozens of potential new types of nonsense. There are too many to discuss, but analyzing a few cases illustrates some underlying general principles. The works of authors like John Taylor, Lewis Carroll, and others are a rich source of examples of unusual, nonsensical figures of speech. Such authors often used figures of speech to enhance the delightful effects of nonsense.

Lewis Carroll's character of Humpty Dumpty is a famous example of how a figure of speech can be transformed into nonsense. Carroll's Humpty Dumpty is a personification of the figure of speech known as aposiopesis. Aposiopesis is breaking off in mid-sentence, leaving a thought suspended in mid-air. For example, an angry farmer says to an intruder, "Get off my land, stranger, or I'll—" Aposiopesis is effective for making veiled threats that leave a lot to the listener's imagination.

Or, just as he dies, a character in a movie says, "I buried the treasure under the—." People die in mid-sentence more often in movies than they do in the real world. Aposiopetic deaths sometimes do occur, though, and they are not merely a literary device.

Or, at a wedding banquet, the groom's father stands to toast his son. He raises his glass, looks at his son, and says, "I am so happy for you, I—" and he breaks down in sobs. In cases like this, aposiopesis indicates that the speaker is choked up with emotion and cannot continue to speak.

Or, a man rambles on and on, talking about his philosophical principles. Finally, an exasperated friend interrupts and says, "And your point is—?" The friend's aposiopetic question is meant to focus the man's attention on some specific thought or topic. An aposiopetic question invites the listener to complete the sentence.

Virtually everyone recognizes those scenarios, and they recognize that pattern of breaking off in mid-sentence as something they have encountered many times in the past. They also acknowledge, though, that they had not thought about it until someone pointed the pattern out to them. And almost nobody knows that it is a figure of speech known as aposiopesis.

They never thought about it before and they never heard the word. Yet, when shown examples of aposiopesis, they instantly recognize them as something they have encountered many times before. That process is the hallmark of the preconscious mind, as it is known to psychiatrists. In other words, the preconscious mind harbors a considerable body of knowledge that people almost never think about consciously. Not only do people harbor preconscious knowledge about aposiopesis, but also about three or four dozen other figures of speech whose names only experts in literature and rhetoric recognize.

Figures of speech in advertising, political rhetoric, literature, drama, courtroom speeches, and news reports resonate strongly with people in their preconscious minds. Hence, figures of speech can enhance the effects of nonsense. Again, Carroll's use of Humpty Dumpty to personify aposiopesis exemplifies how a figure of speech can be transmuted into nonsense. Humpty Dumpty recited a nonsense poem with several aposiopetic lines, such as:

> The little fishes' answer was
> 'We cannot do it, Sir, because—'
>
> ...
>
> And he was very proud and stiff:
> He said, 'I'd go and wake them, if—'
>
> ...
>
> And when I found the door was shut,
> I tried to turn the handle, but—[34]

---

34   Carroll, *Through the Looking-Glass*, 130, 132.

Nothing in the context of the poem gives any clue as to what might conceivably follow the dashes and complete the sentences. Readers are left with no basis for imagining, even vaguely, what the missing information might be.

Humpty Dumpty is an ideal character for personifying this type of figurative nonsense, for when no intelligible basis is provided for reconstructing what sort of thing might follow the interruption, an aposiopesis can become nonsensical. In other words, there is no way to put a sentence that is a nonsensical aposiopesis back together again. Similarly, it is impossible to put a broken egg like Humpty Dumpty back together again.

In scenarios such as the farmer who menaced the stranger or the father at his son's wedding, we can plausibly guess what sort of thing the speaker might have said next. In routine cases like those, an aposiopesis is intelligible, meaningful, and makes sense. However, the poem "Humpty Dumpty," recited, excludes any hint as to how the aposiopetic sentences might be completed, and that made the sentences aposiopetic nonsense.

A literary critic who highly praised Carroll's work nonetheless singled out Humpty Dumpty's poem for some harsh words. He said that this particular poem is "not good nonsense."[35] Similarly, my students reported that the poem grated on their nerves, perhaps because of the repeated interruptions.

---

35   From Carroll and Gardner, *Annotated Alice*.

This kind of analysis could be made for many other figures of speech that writers like Lewis Carroll used nonsensically. For instance, Algernon Charles Swinburne (1837–1909) used alliteration to augment the effect of categorical nonsense in his poem "Nephelidia." The title echoes the Greek word for clouds, and Swinburne's alliteration magnifies the cloudy, misty, smoky, confusing effect categorical nonsense has on the mind. The lines below are typical of the poem:

> From the depth of the dreamy decline of the dawn through
> a notable nimbus of nebulous noonshine,
> Pallid and pink as the palm of the flag-flower that flickers
> with fear of the flies as they float.[36]

Metaphor is often cited as the quintessential figure of speech. Metaphors are figurative comparisons; they compare one thing to another disparate thing. We can understand a metaphor because we can potentially translate it into an equivalent literal meaning. If no equivalent literal meaning can be provided, an attempted metaphor lapses into categorical nonsense. Concrete examples below illustrate this principle:

> Aunt Florene is a pillar of her community.

> Uncle Hamperd is a pig.

> Their son Lester is a time bomb.

> Their house is an excrescence on the landscape.

---

36 Swinburne, "Nephelidia," 245.

CHAPTER 2

The meanings of the metaphors above are transparent. We could rework each metaphor into more literal words that mean the same thing. We could substitute literal meanings for the metaphors.

> Aunt Florene reliably helps others in her community, and they respect and look up to her.

> Uncle Hamperd is lazy, greedy, and slovenly, and he eats too much food.

> Their son Lester is an angry person who is bound to act out violently someday.

> Their house is run-down and decrepit and surrounded by junk and high weeds in the yard.

Metaphors like these make sense to everyone. No problems arise when we try to rephrase them in literal terms. Sometimes the situation is not so straightforward. Consider the following sentences:

> Aunt Florene is an ethereal banana.

> Uncle Hamperd is a prancing abstraction.

> Their son Lester is an iridescent equation.

> Their house is a total potato.

The sentences look like metaphors. They are striking because they are puzzling, though, not because they express an interesting insight. The sentences show that when metaphors cannot be backed by literal equivalents, they turn into categorical nonsense.

To recap, understanding figurative meanings depends on being able to specify equivalent literal meanings. During the Watergate crisis, people instantly understood John Dean's graphic metaphor, "A cancer is growing on the presidency." Yet, unless one knows relevant background information, the metaphor appears to be categorical nonsense, for a governmental institution cannot have a physical ailment.

Similes are also figurative comparisons. Unlike metaphors, though, similes use the words "like" or "as" to make the comparison explicit. My favorite nonsense poem is composed primarily of unintelligible similes. Bishop Richard Corbet (1582–1635) wrote this astonishing work to serve as his epitaph. Each of its three stanzas consists of four nonsensical similes and ends in a self-contradiction. The first stanza is as follows:

> Like to the thundering tone of unspoke speeches.
> Or like a lobster clad in logic breeches.
> Or like the gray fur of a crimson cat.
> Or like the mooncalf in a slipshod hat;
> E'en such is he who never was begotten
> Until his children were both dead and rotten.[37]

---

37 Corbet, "Like to the Thundering Tone," 27.

CHAPTER 2

Soraismic Language

Soraism is a figure of speech that mixes elements of more than one language, which sounds like a recipe for incomprehension, yet some soraisms do make sense. Consider the following sentence:

> Hey, *garçon,* pour some more *eau* in my glass and bring *moi deux* more of those fried *oeufs, s'il vous plait.*

Anyone who understood both French and English would grasp the speaker's meaning. Sentences like these may indicate ignorance or affectation, but at least they are meaningful and intelligible. Other times, however, soraisms are meaningless, unintelligible nonsense. For example, consider the following sentence:

> *Moi, deux* some fried *belle* in *garçon,* and *eoufs* those my glass, *s'il vous plait.*

This sentence is meaningless nonsense to those who speak both languages. Accordingly, soraismic nonsense is a meaningless, unintelligible admixture of elements from two different languages. Writers sometimes use this formula deliberately to create nonsense.

Usually writers who create soraismic nonsense do so for its comic effect. For example, Edward Lear wrote a funny soraismic nonsense poem called "The Cummerbund." The poem mixes English with words he heard while traveling in India. I placed an English translation beside each Indian word in the excerpt printed below. That way, it is easy to see that

the combined effect of the English words and Indian words
is nonsense.

> She Sat upon her Dobie [washerman]
> To watch the Evening Star
> And all the Punkahs [fan] as they passed
> Cried, "My! how fair you are!"
> Around her bower, with quivering leaves.
> The tall Kamsamahs [butler] grew,
> And Kitmutgars [waiter at table] in wild festoons
> Hung down from Tchokis [police or post station] blue.[38]

EXERCISE

Soraismic Nonsense

Moi, deux, some fried belle in garcon and eoufs those my glass, s'il vous plait.

1. Write an example of soraismic nonsense, mixing English and any other language with which you are familiar.

2. Introspect, then record your feelings and impressions about the mental process of writing soraismic nonsense.

---

38   Lear, "The Cummerbund," 25–26.

Faux Language

Faux language is meaningless verbiage that mimics the phonetic characteristics of an actual known language. Faux language can be made to sound like French, English, Italian, German, Chinese, or any other desired language.

Faux language is most common in the context of comedy. For example, the Swedish Chef, Jim Henson's Muppet character, chortles joyfully in faux Swedish. His chortling sounds like Swedish to Americans and to others who do not speak Swedish. However, a Swedish student told me that the Swedish chef's speech does not sound like Swedish to her. She likes the character, though, and he makes her laugh.

Similarly, I heard a French comedian entertain an audience in Paris with a funny nonsense version of English. Although it was hilarious, his faux English did not sound like English to me. Obviously, it sounded like English to his French audience, however.

Faux language is usually a parody or satire of the known language it mimics. It pokes fun at a language or at the people who speak that language. Accordingly, the grammar and vocabulary of the language are immaterial. What is important is that the sound of the faux language is similar to that of a known language. Thus, comedians speaking faux language often toss in a few actual words of the known language to enhance the illusion.

Mock Languages

Farizi

> Jamastapozortin potara nefexi armasparizironarok:
> Noharbitorogonoki abraza gefek ozokokomastangiti.
> Spodotifolonihonik oprana ufeki spozizomomaskargiti.

Nuffish

> Undee glunk bemummy dee gog charch posit
> mezazzle um nunch toof meluster clatch. Dem
> hobbib bezazzie potis, mulk teeka toof, um dee
> roofus dee min tibbles. Bondo. Ne mim ribble mo
> rast. Tumbummy! Dee gon konka dack um ribble
> mepaddy, unka diff dee somplety flookerdash.

A mock language is meaningless, unintelligible verbiage that is invented to look or sound like an unknown language. I wrote the passage below in "Bongonese" to serve as example. Bongonese looks and sounds like a language, but really there is no such language.

> Hobbanopu nopoummum humbummum wum
> bumspummum. Ogga moonbam ugga gomgom,
> num wumbum wommawooba wobbnuppu
> onggom obba nopopummum nuppa gomgom
> nuppatuppa wooma wumwamma oggagom.

Mock languages provide us with no means of interpreting them. That is, we have no method of determining whether or not these passages are grammatically correct. Nor are there dictionaries in which we could look up the words to find out what they mean or check the spelling. Hence, at first, these mock languages seem beyond the pale.

Upon reflecting, however, we realize that mock languages have some basic structural features of known languages. They are written in the letters of the Roman alphabet. They are apparently divided into sentences. They are punctuated with ordinary punctuation marks, and the letters are grouped into small units that look like words.

Each maintains its own distinctive characteristics throughout the whole passage. Furthermore, many more mock languages are possible, each one unique and distinctive.

Writers create mock languages for works of fiction, including novels and movies. Mock languages represent the supposed languages of fictional tribes, beings from outer space, or, sometimes, animals. Thus, mock languages are common in science fiction.

Hence, we need to distinguish mock languages from artificial languages. The Klingon language of Star Trek, for example, is an artificial language. It has a grammar and vocabulary, and speakers who know it can use it to communicate. Indeed, some Star Trek fans speak Klingon among themselves, and there are Klingon dictionaries in which they can look up words. Artificial languages are unlike mock languages, for mock languages are devoid of grammar, vocabulary, or meaning.

John Taylor, Edward Lear, and other nonsense poets created mock languages, although Lewis Carroll never did. To demonstrate the typical characteristics of mock language, here is a passage of mock language by John Taylor from "Epitaph in the Bermuda Tongue":

> Hough gruntough wough Thornough/
> Coratough, Odcough robunquogh.[39]

Mock Language

Jamatapozortin potara nefexi armasparizrok. No harbitoronoga abrazan gefeko opranoto zamagiti.

Undee glunk bemummy dee gog charch posit mezazzle meluster gatch. Ne mimribble mo rast.

1. Write an original example of mock language.

2. Introspect, then record your feelings and impressions about the mental process of writing mock language.

---

39 Reynolds, *Radical Children's Literature*, 46.

CHAPTER 2

Nonsense Stories

Nonsense can be built around the framework of a story or narrative. That is, meaningless, unintelligible language can be put together in the form of stories, and the nonsense stories that result produce a curious, dreamlike sense of narrative action. British actor Samuel Foote wrote the following nonsense story in the 1750s:

> So she went into the garden to cut a cabbage leaf, to make an apple-pie; and at the same time a great she-bear, coming up the street, pops its head into the shop. "What? No soap?" So he died, and she very imprudently married the barber; and there were present the Picninnies, and the Joblillies, and the Garyulies, and the grand Panjandrum himself, with the little round button on top; and they all fell to playing the game of catch as catch can, till the gunpowder ran out at the heels of their boots.[40]

Foote wrote the story to challenge Charles Macklin, a retired actor who boasted that he could repeat anything from memory after hearing it just once. Foote's story proved Macklin wrong. Nevertheless, the story is easy to memorize upon several re-readings. Hence, doctors once used Foote's nonsense story to test their patients' memory.

Playground rhymes often tell nonsense stories. Groups of children chant playground rhymes to create a beat for games, such as jumping rope or tossing a ball. Such rhymes are transmitted from child to child, with only minor alterations,

---

40   Benham, *A Book of Quotations, Proverbs and Household Words*, 449.

for decades and decades, yet each succeeding generation of children believes that they themselves created those venerable verses. Playground rhymes integrate nonsense, meaningful words, narrating a story, and repetitive physical activity. Here is an example:

> I went to the movies tomorrow
> And took a front seat at the back.
> I fell from the floor to the balcony
> And broke a front bone in my back.

These nonsense stories consist mostly of self-contradictions that cancel themselves out. Reading the stories does create some sense of progressing from one action or event to the next, as in an intelligible story. Another famous playground rhyme incorporates the same pattern of a series of self-contradictions to tell a nonsense story, as we shall see later.

Another subtype of nonsense stories works by defying basic conventions of narrative structure. A closed loop of meaningless language can create an illusion of progression by going around in the same endless circle. A PhD student of cognitive psychology recited this example to me:

It was a cold night on the mountaintop, and the cow-
boys were huddled around a campfire. Suddenly, one of
them spoke up and said, "Tell us a tale, Luke." So, this
is the tale that Luke told.

It was a cold night on the mountaintop, and the cow-
boys were huddled around a campfire. Suddenly, one of
them spoke up and said, "Tell us a tale, Luke." So, this
is the tale that Luke told.

It was a cold night on the mountaintop and the cow-
boys huddled around a campfire. Suddenly, one of them
spoke up and said, "Tell us a tale, Luke." So, this is the
tale that Luke told. Etcetera, etcetera, etcetera.

How do nonsense narratives create these crazy effects?
Throughout life, most people love stories, and we tell stories to children from their earliest years. So, in childhood,
we soon internalize the basic abstract framework that under-
lies all stories. The basic narrative framework then vanishes
into the background and operates automatically. Afterwards,
we do not think about the basic structural constituents of
narratives when we are absorbed in enjoyable stories. Therefore, when meaningless, unintelligible language is laid out
over the framework of a story, it creates a sense of narrative
action. Here again we see that the form of language takes
precedence when there is no meaning.

Nonsense Stories

One bright day in the middle of the night, two dead boys got up to fight.

Back to back they faced each other, drew their swords, and shot each other.

A deaf policeman heard the noise and came and killed the two dead boys.

1. Write an original nonsense story.

2. Introspect, then record your feelings and impressions about the mental process of writing a nonsense story.

. . . .

The next type of nonsense is a subtype of nonsense stories. However, it has certain extraordinary characteristics and effects that deserve separate consideration. Therefore, it seems best to put the strange case of nonsense in motion into its own category.

Nonsense Travel Narratives

Nonsense language can be structured to create an illusory sense of motion in the mind. Abraham Lincoln used this device to make people laugh when things went wrong at a solemn state ceremony. His role in the ceremony called for him to ride away from the scene on horseback, leading a procession.

When Mr. Lincoln climbed into the saddle, the horse lifted up its hind leg and got its hoof caught in the stirrup. As the horse hopped around helplessly, the crowd was embarrassed into silence by seeing the President in such an undignified predicament. But Mr. Lincoln looked down at the horse and said, "Well, if you're getting on, I'm getting off."

The motion the joke contemplates cannot take place, except in words. A horse cannot get onto its own back by putting its hoof into a stirrup and climbing into the saddle, yet Mr. Lincoln's words create in the mind a vivid, though confused and incoherent, image of that very motion.

Fiction and nonfiction travelogues are a perennially popular form of literature for old and young people alike. Children are exposed to travel narratives at a young age. Thereafter, children love to listen to travel stories and read them and see them in movies.

Concurrently, early in life, almost everyone develops the basic verbal skill of recounting journeys and telling stories of one's travels. The narrative format itself soon becomes automatic, and the speaker just supplies the specifics of the story. In sum, the travel narrative format is ubiquitous and so familiar from such an early age that it recedes into the background. Normally we do not even think about it.

Its strong appeal and deeply ingrained familiarity make the format of a travel narrative an excellent vehicle for nonsense writing. Laying nonsense out as a travel narrative produces a strange mental sense of motion. In their minds, those reading or listening to a nonsense travel narrative experience a kind of motion that cannot take place, except in words. Nonsensical travel tales lead us on fascinating mental journeys.

In my courses and workshops, participants introspected as they listened to, or read, nonsense travel narratives. Throughout the exercise, they remained aware that the poems were unintelligible nonsense, yet they experienced a strong inner sense of motion. One can appreciate these effects simply by introspecting while reading nonsense travelogues. A nineteenth-century example called "An Unsuspected Fact" follows:

> If down his throat a man should choose
> In fun, to jump or slide,
> He'd scrape his shoes against his teeth,
> Nor dirt his own inside.[41]

---

41 Cannon, "An Unsuspected Fact," 242.

CHAPTER 2

Nonsense Worlds

Almost every child develops the basic verbal skill of describing a place. Place descriptions are ubiquitous in literature, in news stories, and in conversation. From constant exposure, almost everyone is familiar with the format, so its ingrained familiarity makes it an excellent vehicle for nonsense writing.

A layer of nonsense may be put down over the conventional framework of a place description. The process creates an illusionary place in the mind that cannot exist other than in words. Complex nonsense place descriptions evoke corresponding nonsense worlds in the mind. While nonsense worlds are nowhere to be seen except in the mind's eye, they are of considerable social and historical significance. We will look at two literary examples of nonsense worlds. The first example is from *Flatland*, a novel by Edwin A. Abbott (1838–1929). Abbott was an Anglican clergyman and lecturer at Cambridge University. *Flatland* is a classic of nonsense writing that evokes a curious alternate world in order to satirize nineteenth-century British society. Within the space of a few paragraphs, the book draws us into a strange two-dimensional realm or state of existence. We quickly find that the strange world is inhabited by sentient geometric figures.

> I call our world Flatland, not because we call it so, but to make its nature clearer to you, my happy readers, who are privileged to live in Space.
>
> Imagine a vast sheet of paper on which straight Lines, Triangles, Squares, Pentagons, Hexagons, and other figures, instead of remaining fixed in their places,

move freely about, on or in the surface, but without the power of rising above or sinking below it, very much like shadows—only hard and with luminous edges— and you will then have a pretty correct notion of my country and countrymen.[42]

Abbott explains that only straight lines are visible in Flatland. There is no source of light, and therefore no shadows are created that could provide a sense of perspective.

If our friend comes closer to us we see his line becomes larger; if he leaves us it becomes smaller: but still he looks like a straight line; be he a Triangle, Square, Pentagon, Hexagon, Circle, what you will—a straight Line he looks and nothing else.[43]

Abbott's book uses categorical nonsense to evoke an alternate reality. For, plainly, imputing thought and a hierarchical society to triangles, squares, and circles mismatches things and attributes. Here we find nonsense superimposed on the format of a place description. The process creates a mental world that cannot be, except in words.

"Turvey Top," a nineteenth-century nonsense poem by William Sawyer, creates an illusory world by using self-contradictions. Like Abbott's book, the poem evokes a nonsense world in order to satirize the existing human world. It pokes fun at humanity's foibles and misplaced values.

---

42 Abbott, *Flatland*, 11.

43 Abbott, *Flatland*, 14.

'Twas after a supper of Norfolk brawn
That into a doze I chanced to drop,
And thence awoke in the gray of dawn,
In the wonder-land of Turvey Top.

A land so strange I never had seen,
And could not choose but look and laugh—
A land where the small the great includes,
And the whole is less than the half!

A land where the circles were not lines
Round central points, as schoolmen show,
And the parallels met whenever they chose,
And went playing at touch-and-go!

There—except that every round was square,
And save that all the squares were round—
No surface had limits anywhere,
So they never could beat the bounds.

In their gardens, fruit before blossom came.
And the trees diminished as they grew;
And you never went out to walk a mile,
It was the mile that walked to you.

The people there are not tall or short,
Heavy or light, or stout or thin,
And their lives begin where they should leave off,
Or leave off where they should begin.[44]

---

44 Sawyer, "Turvey Top," 474.

ExERciSE

Introspect and Answer These Questions

1. Which type of nonsense did you like best? Which did you like least or dislike? Why?

2. What was your mental process of switching from one type of nonsense to writing another type? Describe your experience.

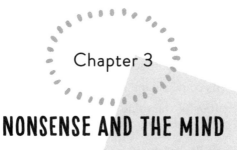

Chapter 3

NONSENSE AND THE MIND

*The pendulum of the mind oscillates
between sense and nonsense, not
between right and wrong.*

C. G. Jung

This chapter uncovers deep connections between nonsense and the mind. A descriptive map of the complex mental causes and effects of nonsense will emerge. Consequently, reading this chapter will bring the hidden, unconscious world of nonsense fully into your conscious mind.

We will learn that nonsense is often a structural element of jokes and humor. We will see that talking nonsense sometimes indicates physical or mental illness. And we will understand some important commercial applications of nonsense, including advertising.

Nonsense is also an important uncharted dimension of the personality. For instance, individuals vary dramatically in their psychological responses to nonsense of various types. Studying the exercises students completed in my courses, I discerned fascinating underlying patterns in their responses. Such patterns convince me that there are distinctive, identifiable capacities of the mind that relate specifically to nonsense.

Carolyn Wells was an eminent literary scholar and expert on nonsense who edited *The Nonsense Anthology* (1905). In the introduction to that work, she said, "A sense of nonsense is as distinct a part of our mentality as a sense of humor." My research convinces me that she was right, for students who completed the exercises thereby demonstrated six latent powers of their minds.

First, they were able to recognize certain examples of written or spoken language as unintelligible, meaningless, and nonsensical.

Second, they could identify nonsense by type.

Third, they could distinguish among different kinds of nonsense according to their distinctive structural characteristics.

Fourth, they could perceive, appreciate, and describe various aesthetic, emotional, and cognitive effects of nonsense.

Fifth, they could write original creative nonsense of practically any type they studied.

NONSENSE AND THE MIND

And sixth, they could identify nonsense they had not studied before and characterize their structures by using the principles of typology they had learned.

These six cognitive and creative capacities are an essential part of our mental makeup, and later on they will prove highly valuable, for we will see that they are critical for thinking logically about some important questions that have long eluded reason. Hence, it is useful to group together these six mental capacities related to unintelligible, meaningless language. Moreover, it is plausible to refer to them collectively as a sense of nonsense. And the sense of nonsense plays central roles in numerous psychological processes, or mental states.

In the meantime, it is simple to awaken the sense of nonsense. Each semester I directly witnessed and monitored positive developmental changes in my students' sense of nonsense. They resumed a developmental process that was apparently stunted as they grew into adulthood. Many students commented that they benefited from taking the course. Even decades later, some have contacted me to say that what they learned about nonsense has helped them in their professional lives. For example, many students have told me that after learning my nonsense logic, it made other apparently unrelated subjects clearer to them.

My sense of nonsense has been an indispensable asset during my career as a medical doctor and psychiatrist, for it often helps me make sense of someone's unique inner experience. Sometimes the nonsense that somebody talks becomes a notable aspect of that individual's personality. The condition known as synesthesia is a case in point.

Synesthesia is the psychological trait of experiencing cross-sensory perceptions. That is, a perception in one sense, such as hearing, automatically and involuntarily produces an accompanying perceptive experience in another sense, such as vision. Hence, hearing a series of sounds will also give rise to an inner experience of seeing colors. Synesthetes (people with synesthesia) are therefore forced to talk nonsense to try and describe their unusual inner worlds. They say things like "Jill's voice is light purple, but Jason's voice is dark green."

Colored hearing is one of the most common forms of synesthesia, but there are several dozen types. Thus, while some synesthetes report experiencing sounds as having colors, others report experiencing colors as having sounds. Dr. Richard Cytowic's book *Synesthesia* (MIT Press, 2018) describes a boy who said things such as "That note is red." The first time the boy saw a rainbow, he exclaimed, "A song, a song!"

Other synesthetes experience tastes as having colors. They talk nonsense like "Coffee tastes dark green, and milk tastes light orange." Yet other synesthetes experience tastes as having shapes. They say nonsensical things like "Beet tastes square, and chicken tastes round."

Synesthesia runs in families; some people experience synesthesia as children but eventually outgrow it. The nonsense that synesthetes talk reveals that their inner worlds are different than those of most other people.

Nonsense is a developmental marker of children's learning of language.

When my son Carter was six months old, my wife read him a book of nonsense poetry for children. Carter's big smile and peals of gleeful laughter were remarkable. To my wife and me, it certainly appeared that Carter appreciated the difference between meaningful language and nonsense. Perhaps independent investigators can confirm or disconfirm that infants can sometimes recognize nonsense.

Either way, though, nonsense enters into children's lives at an early age. For instance, nonsense plays a role in the acquisition of language. Children three to six years of age make up nonsense words for fun as an expression of humor and their creative spirit.

The pleasure children take in making up meaningless words indicates that they have attained a certain level of understanding of language, for they must possess a large vocabulary of meaningful words to appreciate their difference from meaningless nonsense words. Furthermore, the nonsense words that children invent reflect the phonetic patterns of words in their own language. English-speaking children's meaningless invented words are near-English nonsense, for example.

Preschoolers talk various forms of numerative nonsense as part of the process of learning numbers. For example, I once saw two kindergartners fighting over a swing at a playground. One yelled, "I'm telling you for the fifty-eleventh time, get off my swing!" Many observant parents can recount similar incidents.

When my son Avery was three years old, he looked at my watch and asked, "Is it timey-till?" When I said, "Well, there is no such time as 'timey-till,'" he asked again, louder, and only stopped when I said yes.

When he was six years old, my son Samuel invented his own nonsensical system of counting. He felt certain that there had to be something before zero, so, first, he would fix his gaze ahead intently for a second or two. Then he would exclaim, "Wait!" And then, "Nothing!" And only then would he say, "Zero!"

My daughter, Carol Ann, also created funny numerative nonsense. When she was five and a half years old, she held a metal tape measure and placed the tip of it near the top of my head. She looked at the tape measure and said, "You are forty-eight pounds tall."

Before she learned to draw the letters of the alphabet, Carol Ann went through a phase of mock writing. Beginning when she was about nine or ten months old, she enjoyed sitting with me as I wrote in my notebooks. When she was three years and two months old, she took the pen herself. She said she was writing as she drew pointed squiggles that exactly resembled the mock writing in cartoons. As she drew, she recited a seemingly random series of letters: "C, E, A, B, T."

When my grandson, Ray, was four years old, he learned the concept of opposites by playing a game of question and answer with his parents. Ray and his parents would ask each other, for example, "What is the opposite of up?" or "What is the opposite of hot?" and "What is the opposite of dark?" Once, when his turn came, Ray asked, "What is the opposite of car?"

Ray's question is an instance of categorical nonsense, another type that we examined earlier. A sentence of categorical nonsense is grammatically correct and all the words are meaningful. However, the concepts in the sentence do not fit together. Hence, children often talk nonsense inadvertently when they are trying to learn a new concept.

These and many other instances show that children create nonsense as they are learning language. A nonsense phrase seems to be a part of the process of learning numbers or how to write or a new concept. Nevertheless, occasional individuals worry that it might be dangerous to read the works of Lewis Carroll and Dr. Seuss to children. They are concerned that nonsense writings could interfere with children's ability to distinguish fact from fantasy.

In reality, however, it seems the very opposite is true. The Russian child psychologist Kornei Chukovsky observed that nonsense actually exerts a beneficial influence on children's sense of reality. He wrote:

> Nonsense...not only does not interfere with the child's orientation to the world that surrounds him, but, on the contrary, strengthens in his mind a sense of the real; and that it is precisely in order to further the education of children in reality that such nonsense verse should

be offered to them…One can cite any number of such [verses] which testify to the inexhaustible need of every healthy child of every era and of every nation to introduce nonsense into his small but ordered world, with which he has only recently become acquainted. Hardly has the child comprehended with certainty which objects go together and which do not, when he begins to listen happily to verses of absurdity.[45]

Nonsense is often humorous: "I am nude under my clothes." The words certainly command attention, and they create a vivid image in the mind, yet the intellect strives in vain to put them together as a meaningful sentence. In other words, the sentence is unintelligible, and that is part of what makes it funny. Anyone who studies the subject soon realizes that there is a strong connection between nonsense and humorous laughter.

Nonsense promotes social bonding. A few nonsensical playground rhymes like the one below have been transmitted virtually unchanged for well over a century. They are a form of oral literature, passed along only by word of mouth from child to child.

> One bright day in the middle of the night
> Two dead boys got up to fight
> Back to back they faced each other,
> Drew their swords and shot each other.
> A blind man came to see the fray.

---

45 Kornei Chukovsky, *From Two to Five* (Berkeley, Los Angeles, London: University of California Press, 1971), translated and edited by Miriam Morton.

A dumb man came to shout "hooray!"
A deaf policeman heard the noise
And came and killed those two dead boys.

Children chant those playground rhymes together, often while tossing a ball around among themselves in a circle. This way of integrating nonsense chanting with physical activity can forge enduring social bonds. Many adults can still recite these nonsense rhymes and have fond childhood memories of chanting them with their friends.

My friend Madeleine Diemer, a psychotherapist, also has warm childhood memories of reciting nonsense with other people to cement a bond with them. Madeline would recite nonsense with her family members. They said these words together each night when they finished eating dinner: "I've had an excellent sufficiency, and more would be prodotony to my apathetic quantity, which is quite quadilified." Since then I have learned of several instances of this among my friends and acquaintances.

Hence, I surmise that the practice of talking nonsense together as a family after dinner must be a more common ritual than I would have imagined. Furthermore, the people who shared these memories with me obviously looked back on their experiences with nostalgic tenderness. Thinking about the nonsense they would recite seemed to stir up their feelings about their family members.

Apparently, group recitations of nonsense are sometimes an effective means of creating social bonds among people.

How this works is not clear, but it is an interesting effect and bears further investigation. Later we will discover more about the use of nonsense to unify people and get them to cooperate with each other.

Nonsense heard from others sometimes prompts people to talk nonsense involuntarily in response. When my children were only three or four years old, they would talk nonsense back to me when I talked nonsense to them. This and other observations lead me to believe that nonsense breeds nonsense. That is, talking nonsense seems to predispose people to respond with nonsense. This happens automatically, without any conscious intention on their part. I could recount about a dozen cases of this effect, of which the following two cases are representative.

I once read this sentence to my assistant:

> The slozy begoners floofed in tarkly from below in their cluddering, plaggering flootiedopters.

The sentence astonished and energized her. She became somewhat agitated and spoke rapidly. She launched into an excited attempt to explain away the sentence. It seemed particularly unsettling to her that flootiedopters would floof in from below. Her explanation quickly ran aground and trailed off into incoherent, unintelligible nonsense.

In another example, my brother and I once stayed up talking most of the night. In the early morning hours, I read him Lewis Carroll's "Jabberwocky" and Algernon C.

Swinburne's "Nephelidia." The nonsense had an astonishing, delayed effect on him. Over the next few days, nonsense would insert itself, uninvited, into his conversations. He said, "For a couple of days afterwards, nonsense was at the front of my mind. Something that wasn't even a real word would enter my mind and fly out of my mouth before I knew what was happening. It was as though I had no control over what I said. Nonsense words would come out in my dreams, too."

What is it about nonsense that seems to inspire nonsense in others? What might we learn about human psychology by investigating this "rebound effect" more carefully and looking at the hidden, powerful qualities of unintelligible speech?

Nonsense sometimes emerges when the mind is attempting to escape from a severe stressor. Severe overwhelming stress makes people talk incoherent nonsense. G. K. Chesterton once said it was the "idea of escape" that is "the idea that lies at the back of all nonsense." Soldiers rescued from horrendous combat situations sometimes could only talk in garbled nonsense afterward. Although they survived uninjured, the soldiers had faced imminent death. The psychological trauma had left them unable to put words together into intelligible sentences.

I observed this phenomenon a few times myself when working as a physician in emergency rooms. Sometimes survivors of horrific accidents would talk incoherent nonsense after they had been brought in from the scene. Though they had not been hurt in the accident, overwhelming stress disrupted their mental processes that organized meaningful speech.

On April 16, 2007, a disturbed gunman shot and killed 32 students and professors at Virginia Tech University. The killer trapped thirty of his victims in a campus building and shot them in the classrooms at point-blank range. Other students survived by jumping to safety from windows on the second floor. One student who escaped telephoned his mother immediately afterwards to assure her that he was safe. She reported that initially he was incoherent when he spoke to her. At first, she said, "I couldn't understand him. It was like gibberish."[46]

Nonsense is inseparably connected with sleeping and dreaming. Hypnagogia is a transitional state of consciousness people experience as they drift from wakefulness to sleep. Many people perceive surrealistic, iridescently colorful mental imagery during the hypnagogic phase of consciousness. Many also experience strange nonsense words and phrases running through their minds.

I have written down my own hypnagogic nonsense since graduate school. I have heard disconnected nonsense phrases such as "fine of apple bijani," "two nose of harsh cumple," "obal summus," and "drish the awesome closerfose." Experts on hypnagogic phenomena recognize this kind of nonsense as a common manifestation of the process of going to sleep.

---

46 *New York Times*, April 17, 2007, A24.

In the superb book *Hypnagogia,* Andreas Mavromatis quotes dozens of similar examples of hypnagogic nonsense from various sources, including:

Lacertina Wain

They are exposed to verbally intellection.

He is as good as cake double.

A leading clerk is a great thing in my profession, as well as a Sabine footertootro.

To the sidewalk with Tell too.

Conceit is not often being named a phantabilit.

A Burul house Schillinger to cook plate.

Amaranda es tifiercia.

Knows how tampala sounds.

Suddenly waking up with a "brilliant" idea is another common hypnagogic experience. People sometimes write down nighttime revelations, then go back to sleep, confident that their discovery will revolutionize the world. Occasionally, these ideas do pan out. More often, though, the sleepers are disappointed the next morning, for they realize that what they wrote during the night is nonsense. Jonathan Swift (1667–1745), who wrote *Gulliver's Travels,* experienced this odd phenomenon. He recorded the following nonsense poem he heard while asleep: "I walk before no man, a hawk in his fist; Nor am I brilliant, whenever I list."[47]

Similarly, some people talk nonsense when they talk in their sleep. I myself have heard several people talk nonsense in their sleep. Other people have told me the same thing about their sleeping children or spouses who talk nonsense in the night.

Sometimes we are forced to talk nonsense in order to verbalize bizarre, outlandish dreams. As an undergraduate student of philosophy, I once dreamed I was holding arguments in my palms. I seemed to be putting interconnected, silvery segments together in my hands when I was reasoning to prove a point. I also had a dream in which two of my relatives and one of my friends were fused incomprehensibly together into a single dream personage. Of course, some dreams are quite literal and can be captured in straightforward, prosaic language. Often enough, though, nonsense stories are the only available means of putting strange dreams into words.

Nonsense can be a sign of medical or psychiatric disorders. People sometimes talk nonsense when they suffer from psychosis or physical ailments that affect the mind. "Word salad" is a form of nonsensical speech found in schizophrenia. Schizophrenics mix made-up, meaningless neologisms with actual words, with the mixture lacking overall sense. I had a patient with paranoid schizophrenia who made up blatantly obscene nonsense words. His long, rambling epis-

---

47   Damrosch, *Jonathan Swift*, 221.

tles were addressed to no one in particular, and they were full of meaningless words like "thuckabussy," "puckcucky," and "fugbucker."

The self-contradictory utterance "I am dead" is a hallmark of the delusional disorder known as the Cotard syndrome. These patients convince themselves that they are dead, and they cannot be swayed by rational arguments to the contrary. Severe psychotic depression causes this delusional belief that one is dead.

Intoxication with various psychoactive substances also causes people to talk nonsense. For example, the anesthetic nitrous oxide, or laughing gas, has this effect. American psychologist William James studied the effects of nitrous oxide by inhaling it himself. He carefully wrote down what he thought at the time were profound mystical revelations. Here is his account of the phenomenon:

> I have sheet after sheet of phrases dictated or written during the intoxication, which to the sober reader seem meaningless drivel, but which at the moment of transcribing were fused in the fire of infinite rationality.[48]
> What's mistake but a kind of take?
> What's nausea but a kind of -ausea?
> Sober, drunk, -unk, astonishment.
> Everything can become the subject of criticism—how criticise without something to criticise?
> Agreement—disagreement!!
> Emotion—motion!!![49]

---

48   James, *The Will to Believe*, 295.

49   Ibid., 296.

By God, how that hurts! By God, how it doesn't hurt!
Reconciliation of two extremes.
By George, nothing but othing!
That sounds like nonsense, but it is pure onsense.
Thought deeper than speech—!
Medical school; divinity school, school! SCHOOL!
Oh my God, oh God, oh God![50]

Mercury poisoning causes irritability, mood swings, and, sometimes, meaningless, rambling speech. In the nineteenth century, mercury was the main ingredient of a fashionable pharmaceutical remedy for depression known as blue mass. Abraham Lincoln took the popular antidepressant and apparently became intoxicated with mercury.

Henry Clay Whitney was an attorney who often traveled a circuit with his friend, the future president. He wrote that he awoke one morning to find Mr. Lincoln sitting up in bed and "talking the wildest and most incoherent nonsense to himself."[51] Fortunately, Mr. Lincoln stopped taking blue mass before he became president because he found it made him "cross."

Even those who by profession are communicators may have moments where lucidity suddenly lapses. As reported in the March 2015 issue of *New Scientist*, Serene Branson, a Los Angeles broadcaster reporting from the Grammy Awards, struggled visibly to speak meaningfully as her lips formed

50 James, *The Will to Believe*, 297.

51 Richardson, *Richardson's Defense of the South*, 471.

the words, "Well a very, very heavy ah heavy duit burtation tonight. We had a very deres dereson. But let's go ahead tarish dereson tasen losh lobitt behind dupet." Branson later described the moments as terrifying, as she could not put together an intelligible sentence. Later, it was determined that a migraine headache was responsible for her disrupted speech. The same year, a Madison, Wisconsin, television anchor, Sarah Carlson, had a small seizure during a broadcast, leaving a confused and disoriented audience to try to make sense of her unintelligible words.

Athletes of all kinds, particularly boxers and football players, also have had instances in which their language has become unintelligible for medical reasons. In many cases the effects are short-lived, but all who witness the delirious speech realize something beyond the normal has occurred, and it leaves a powerful impression.

Nonsense can make people doubt their senses or think that they are going crazy. Nonsense can confuse people. For instance, double-talk is a variety of near-English nonsense that mentalists and magicians use for entertaining their audiences. They talk double-talk to cloud people's minds and make them laugh.

Double-talk is created by a simple formula: Begin sentences with phrases like, "Do you know—?" or "Will you please tell me—?" or "Do you have any idea where—?" to get listeners' attention. Their wheels start turning as they prepare to come up with an answer. Then toss in a liberal quantity of made-up, meaningless near-English nonsense words. The process results in double-talk such as, "Would you please tell me where I can find some spanagloap for the tarkerblay?"

As listeners, we bring multiple meanings and associations to the act of listening, assuming that in every act of communication, the speaker's intent is to communicate meaningfully. In the case of double-talk, the listener's expectations are not met, and this can lead to people questioning both their senses and sanity.

Nonsense can powerfully attract and hold people's attention. Nonsense often captures and holds attention more effectively than humdrum, prosaic language that is perfectly meaningful and intelligible. For example, advertising is all about getting attention. That is the reason why nonsense shows up frequently in ads. A television ad for KPMG, a corporate finance firm, was built around categorical nonsense. The ad incomprehensibly mixed the phraseology of motherly admonitions with the terminology of international finance. In the ad, cranky mother figures offered meaningless advice like, "Don't go out with wet hair. You might catch a case of involuntary international corporate rightsizing." Another cranky mother insisted, "Always construct a mass utilization model before crossing the street."

Television cable companies compete with operators of television communications satellites. Satellites formerly did not transmit local television news programs, and cable operators saw this as a selling point for their companies. One cable company drove the point home with an ad featuring nonsense in the form of an alien mock language. In the ad, an extraterrestrial sat behind a news desk in a television studio on a distant planet. He delivered the news by chirping away in a nonsense mock language. The ad implied, "If you want to watch the local news, get cable."

The Partnership for a Drug-Free America urges parents to learn about drug abuse to protect their children. The organization spread their message with a television ad that featured a meaningless string of words. In the ad, a concerned mother tries to discuss the drug problem with her teenage daughter, saying, "Hypnosis completely tailwind sowing elephants plant before cartoon paper cups. So numbers renovate. Afterwards lightly fish scale doorbell." Her teenage daughter's facial expression was one of dazed incomprehension, and that drove home the ad's point: namely, get educated on the drug problem before you talk to your children about it. Otherwise, what you say may sound like nonsense to them.

• • • •

Nonsense irresistibly compels some people to search for a supposed hidden meaning. Nonsense drives some people to try to interpret it out of existence. That is, its meaningless, unintelligible quality is beckoning. Nonsense makes us feel that although we cannot discern a meaning, one is somehow just out of reach. We seem to sense a meaning just around the corner or over the horizon. We feel that if we only put in more effort, we may discover this tantalizing meaning, so we turn nonsense over and over in our minds. We try hard to find a position in which the nonsense will snap into place and make sense. Some people go on and on, obsessively working on nonsense, trying to shear as much of the "non" away from it as they can.

These people become fixated on the idea that nonsense is a code, something like pig Latin. If only one could discover its secret formula, nonsense would reveal a hidden message.

The centuries-old Voynich manuscript is a case in point. This bizarre document is kept in the rare books department of the library of Yale University. The two-hundred-plus pages of the manuscript are written in an unintelligible alphabet of twenty-two nonsense letters. The writing resembles no known alphabet.

The margins of the pages are adorned with sketches that resemble those found in medieval illuminated manuscripts. The drawings depict nude women, animals and plants of no known species, and an incomprehensible plumbing system. One commentator said that the "manuscript has the eerie quality of a perfectly sensible book from an alternate universe."

A long parade of cryptographers tried to decipher the Voynich manuscript by assuming that it is in code. The problem is that each cryptographer's solution diverges wildly from all the rest, for the Voynich manuscript is an ingenious hoax and a masterpiece of mock language. Sadly, however, the identity of the clever nonsense writer who dreamed it up is lost in the mists of time.

This is a good place to reflect and remember what nonsense is; namely, it is meaningless, unintelligible language. From the viewpoint of an author trying to write good nonsense poems or stories, accidentally meaning something is a failure of art. Nonsense writers have been bemused by determined enthusiasts who tried to interpret their literary nonsense out of existence by uncovering a concealed meaning in it.

Lewis Carroll was perplexed and amused by his many interpreters. He responded to those who asked him to reveal the supposed hidden meaning of his nonsense poem "The Hunting of the Snark." He wrote:

> I was walking on a hill-side, alone, one bright summer day, when suddenly there came into my head one line of verse—one solitary line—'For the Snark was a Boojum, you see.' I knew not what it meant, then: I know not what it means, now: but I wrote it down: and, some time afterwards, the rest of the stanza occurred to me, that being its last line: and so by degrees, at odd moments during the next year or two, the rest of the poem pieced itself together, that being its last stanza. And since then, periodically, I have received courteous letters from strangers, begging to know whether 'the Hunting of the Snark' is an allegory, or contains some hidden moral, or is a political satire: and for all such questions I have but one answer, "I don't know!"[52]

---

52   Carroll, "Alice on the Stage," 181.

We need to reemphasize that nonsense is not a coded message, for a coded message looks like meaningless, unintelligible nonsense, to be sure. Nevertheless, knowing the code used enables someone to decipher the message and understand its hidden meaning.

Transmitting meaningful, secret messages securely is the purpose of encryption. If the message were meaningless, there would be no need to conceal the meaning. However, by definition, nonsense is meaningless. Therefore, equating nonsense with coded messages destroys the meaning of the word "code" and the meaning of the word "nonsense."

Senders sometimes insert nonsense words into a secret message before encoding it. The technique deceives code-breakers because they look for the *meaning* in a coded message, not for the nonsense in it. In other words, nonsense planted deliberately in coded messages can make the work of deciphering them harder.

Nonsense stimulates a flow of odd mental imagery, half-formed ideas, and fragmentary chains of thought. Nonsense is language that is meaningless and unintelligible by definition, yet something strange and hard to define emerges in the mind of someone who reads nonsense or listens to it being read or spoken aloud. Nonsense can register in the mind as a peculiar, surreal state of consciousness.

Reflecting on a nonsense poem that she heard, Alice said, "Somehow it seems to fill my head with ideas—only I don't know exactly what they are!"[53]

---

53   Carroll, *Through the Looking-Glass*, 34.

My students described their introspective experiences of reading or hearing nonsense in similar terms. According to their descriptions, nonsense induces a stream of incoherent, dreamlike ideation. Nonsense evoked nebulous mentation that they found hard to describe. Nonsense called up garbled images or vague thoughts in their minds.

This off state of free-floating consciousness is the flip side of what happens in the hypnagogic state, dreams, psychosis, and delirium. Those conditions are alternate states of consciousness during which people talk nonsense, and apparently the same process works in the opposite direction. Talking nonsense to people makes them experience a curious, hard-to-describe alternate state of consciousness. In sum, nonsense is an alternate state of language that can induce an alternate state of consciousness.

Does nonsense of each different type induce a corresponding, different alternate state of consciousness? Could a typology of nonsense provide a vocabulary for talking more intelligibly and precisely about alternate states of consciousness? Might some particular type or combination of types of nonsense induce an alternate state of consciousness that would somehow be superior to ordinary consciousness? In other words, could nonsense be a doorway to a higher sense? The universal structural formula that abides in every type of nonsense may help us understand the language of transcendent consciousness.

Chapter 4

NONSENSE AS A HIGHER FORM OF LANGUAGE

Nonsense is not nourished by nonsense but by "sense."

Naomi Lewis

Nonsense supervenes on ordinary language that is meaningful and intelligible. The prefix "non" presents a false picture of nonsense as an inchoate nothingness, and it gives a misleading impression that nonsense is merely the absence of meaning. However, we have seen that nonsense is a complex, intricately structured form of language in its own right.

Nonsense is made up of the same elements that ordinary, intelligible language is. Namely, nonsense consists of sounds, letters, syllables, words, sentences, and so on. Nonsense is rule-governed, as meaningful language is. The departure that makes certain language nonsense is that it follows some rules and breaks other rules in a combination that is unintelligible.

Consequently, in a certain respect, nonsense is more complex than the meaningful, intelligible speech from which it arises and upon which it is founded. To comprehend or elucidate meaningful, intelligible language, we need only to understand the linguistic rules it follows. To comprehend or elucidate unintelligible nonsense, though, we must understand both the rules it follows and the rules it breaks. Accordingly, though, nonsense presents more complicated challenges to the mind than ordinary, meaningful language does.

This inherent complexity makes nonsense a second tier of language, an upper level built on top of ordinary, intelligible language. Hence, nonsense, which is a meaningless, unintelligible, supervenient form of language, might sometimes be in a position to become a higher form of language.

Earlier, we saw that nonsense participates in various transitions. For instance, nonsense occurs in learning a language, drifting from wakefulness into sleep, and escaping to safety from a life-threatening situation. Because it follows some rules and breaks other rules, nonsense is like Janus, the Roman deity who had two faces, one on each side of his head. Janus was the god of such transitions as going from past to future, from one state to another state, and even from one world to another.

Janus was the god of the gate, so he was portrayed with his doorkeeper's key and a staff. With his two faces, he watched over entrances and exits, and he saw both the external world and the internal world. Nonsense, with its dual nature, is similarly associated with transitions and entranceways.

The basic structural formula that undergirds all nonsense is of vital importance, for it accounts for nonsense's curious dual nature. Furthermore, it has two thought-provoking implications.

First, nonsense makes no sense because other language does make sense. Nonsense is made from elements of ordinary language that do have meaning. Therefore, there could be no nonsense unless there were some meaningful, intelligible language from which to make it. Nonsense needs the stable structure of ordinary, intelligible language in order to contrast it, for it is only against the background of intelligible and meaningful speech that we can make the judgment that certain other language is nonsense.

Second, nonsense and unintelligibility can be comprehended by reason. Reason and nonsense are direct opposites, so there is an apparent paradox in the whole notion of studying nonsense and taking the subject seriously. One might well object that rational inquiry into nonsense is a self-contradictory and incoherent quest. After all, by definition, nonsense is something meaningless and unintelligible. How could reason apply to something that makes no sense whatsoever and is intrinsically unintelligible?

The universal structural formula of nonsense resolves the seeming paradox. Although nonsense itself is unintelligible, the structural formula that undergirds all nonsense is an intelligible and rationally discernible principle. This has the surprising consequence that unintelligibility itself is an intelligible phenomenon of language and the mind.

The dual structure of nonsense implies that unintelligibility is a two-part mental process, for the mind must subject language to some sort of process just to ascertain that it is unintelligible. Something unintelligible cannot thwart the intellect without somehow first engaging the intellect. Nonsense engages the intellect with elements of intelligible language and by following some linguistic rules. Meanwhile, however, nonsense thwarts the intellect by breaking other linguistic rules. As a result of it following some rules and breaking others, nonsense is unintelligible language.

It follows that nonsense is not formless, and that even meaningless, unintelligible language has rationally discernible rules attached to it. All of the distinct types of nonsense reflect a single unifying structural essence that reason can discover. Therefore, nonsense is a rationally knowable state of language and the mind.

Nonsense is an innate faculty of the mind. An influential academic theory holds that human beings are born preprogrammed for language. Now we realize that nonsense supervenes on meaningful language, so wherever there is language, there is also the potential for nonsense. Nonsense always follows on the heels of meaningful, intelligible language. Therefore, if the influential academic theory is true, the mind has an inborn capacity to create and be affected by nonsense in certain predictable ways. If humans are born preprogrammed for language, then they are born preprogrammed for nonsense, too.

Is that why nonsense sometimes seems uncannily appropriate to certain entities in the extralinguistic world? For an experiment, psychologist Wolfgang Köhler coined the nonsense words "malooma" and "tikiti." He coined them expressly as meaningless, unintelligible nonsense words to be used in the experiment. First he showed the words to his subjects, then he showed them two drawings. One looked like a fork with spikes and an angular, sharp quality to it. The other was more rounded and had no hard edges. Köhler asked the following question: Which one is the malooma and which one is the tikiti?

More than 90 percent replied that the fork figure was the tikiti and the rounded figure was the malooma. Perhaps this uniform response has to do with synesthesia, the blending of the senses, for the sound of "malooma" is smooth, as are the contours of the rounded figure, whereas the sound of "tikiti" is sharp and spiky, like the fork figure.

Apparently, nonsense can sometimes be a sort of transitional sense, or a trans-sense. We already saw that nonsense is inherent in the mind. Next we will see that nonsense is also an inherently spiritual phenomenon.

Nonsense sometimes interacts with meaningful language to produce synergistic effects. Doo-wop is a form of popular music that originated in the United States in the early 1950s. Doo-wop uses nonsense syllables as harmony, or as the main line of a song. Doo-wop songs contain meaningful words along with the nonsense. In fact, the effect of a doo-wop song depends partly on the balance it strikes between nonsense and meaningful language.

Incidentally, in doo-wop songs, nonsense syllables and meaningful words combined are more forceful and memorable than either is alone. That is, nonsense sometimes acts synergistically with intelligible language to produce enhanced combined effects. Another example is the synergistic use of meaningless refrains in certain enduring nursery rhymes.

> Hickory, dickory, dock
> The mouse ran up the clock
> The clock struck one
> The mouse ran down
> Hickory, dickory, dock

This nursery rhyme is so famous that millions of English-speaking people know it by heart. In an exercise, my students recited the rhyme together as a group to observe how nonsense interacts with intelligible language. First, they recited the rhyme in its entirety. Then, after a brief pause, they recited only the three intelligible lines of the rhyme, namely:

The mouse ran up the clock
The clock struck one
The mouse ran down

All the students were already very familiar with the nursery rhyme from their childhoods, and they understood that it is centuries old. When they recited the three meaningful lines alone, they instantly realized that the beloved rhyme falls flat without its nonsensical refrain, for the meaningless line "hickory, dickory, dock" at the beginning and the end adds energy to the rhyme.

Reciting the line "hickory, dickory, dock" by itself has a pleasant, musical quality, but without the meaningful lines, it is nonsense hanging in a void. This was how the students comprehended that nonsense and intelligible language sometimes have greater power working together than either of them has working alone.

Shamans in preliterate cultures also apparently understood the same principle. Shaman songs consisted of nonsense syllables and meaningless refrains that were integrated with segments of meaningful, intelligible language. In a later chapter, we will see how shamans sang these songs to induce transformative states of consciousness.

Cross-Dimensional Nonsense

Can human consciousness enter a more inclusive state of existence or a higher dimension? If so, what is it like to experience a change of dimension? These questions are key to understanding the meaning of mystical experiences and other supposedly transcendent states of consciousness. The following argument suggests that a mental transition between dimensions would compel somebody to talk nonsense to describe the experience. Consider a popular drawing by graphic artist M. C. Escher. In the drawing, a stream of water falls from high above over a mill wheel. From there, the stream of water then makes several sharp turns in succession through a series of troughs, flowing consistently downward the entire way. At the end of this downward course, though, the water is again high above the mill wheel, where it originated, rendering that sequence of events unintelligible nonsense.

Now, we could intelligibly describe the two-dimensional surface of this drawing. We could use a ruler, a protractor, and a value scale of all shades from dark black to bright white. We could measure the lengths and angles of all the lines that make up the drawing, then we could characterize the shade of every area of the surface. The task would be time-consuming, but it would result in a precise, meaningful description of the two-dimensional drawing.

However, we cannot intelligibly describe the scene that appears in the drawing. Trying to describe what happens in the scene forces us to talk nonsense. In other words, the mind produces nonsense when it switches from one framework of existence to another framework of existence. We could refer to this type of meaningless, unintelligible language as cross-dimensional nonsense. Are there definitive hallmarks of cross-dimensional nonsense? If we can answer that question, perhaps we can detect when someone's mind passes into a transcendent state of existence, and that brings us to the spiritual implications of nonsense.

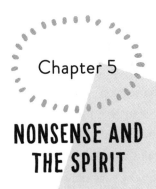

Chapter 5

NONSENSE AND THE SPIRIT

Nonsense is an assertion of man's
spiritual freedom in spite of all
the oppressions of circumstance.

Aldous Huxley

This chapter will look at some sacred texts, doctrines, and practices that reflect the spiritual significance of nonsense. Deliberate nonsense has long been an effective device in various holy writings. We will also see how nonsense is used in certain spiritual traditions for inducing transcendent or mystical states of consciousness.

The first chapter characterized nonsense as primarily a recreational and literary use of language. The shift from recreation to spirituality may seem shocking, for spirituality is a serious, sacred, solemn thing. Recreation, by contrast, is for entertainment, amusement, fun, and relaxation. People usually value their spiritual concerns at a higher level than they value recreation and entertainment, yet the relationship is richer and more complex than ordinarily recognized. Nonsense also comes into play in certain interactions between spirituality and recreation. All three themes come together and illuminate a venerable form of sacred writing known as the abecedarius, or abecedary.

The abecedary is a work of prose or poetry where each line begins with a different successive letter of the alphabet. The abecedary originated as a spiritual practice of writing that was devoted solely to holy purposes and meant exclusively for communicating with divinities or for propounding sacred prophecies. Around a dozen abecedaries are found in the Old Testament, including, for instance, Psalm 119.

In that era each letter had its own spiritual significance, and it was thought that the order of the alphabet was divinely ordained. The abecedary was holy writing that harnessed the mystical powers of all the letters of the alphabet at once. In Revelation Jesus says, "I am the Alpha and the Omega." Jesus's words allude directly to the spiritual powers of abecedaries.

Today, for Jesus or anyone else to say "I am an abecedary" would be nonsensical, for abecedaries have lost their original sacred luster. They are known now mostly as alphabet books for entertaining children as they learn their ABCs.

The mesmerizing power of the abecedary arises from its blending of opposites. The iron-clad order of the alphabet contrasts agreeably with the continuing element of surprise. Readers know what letter will come next, but they cannot know what that letter will bring with it. The same enthralling formula explains the irresistible power of the abecedary in both its forms—spiritual and recreational.

Nonsense that is cast in an abecedarian format projects that same mesmerizing power and has become a frequent structural element of popular abecedaries for children. The immense entertainment value of the abecedary persists when the content is unintelligible nonsense. Numerous amusing and sometimes mind-bending nonsensical abecedaries are always in print.

Priscilla and Whitney Turner built on the format to create their phenomenal book *The War Between the Vowels and the Consonants*. Their story harmonizes nonsense, entertainment, spiritual values, and the ancient theme of balancing order and chaos. The story envisions the alphabet as a world in itself that is populated by intelligent letters. In their alphabet world, elite vowels dominate and suppress the common herd of consonants. Social tensions escalate until there is armed conflict and a civil war breaks out. Unexpectedly, a menacing intruder appears on the horizon of the alphabet world. The horrible intruder is an unintelligible scribbling and scrawling chaos. The warring parties are forced to renounce their conflict to repel the invading unintelligible scrawling and scribbling. Consonants and vowels unite to spell out a big sign that says, "Go away, you silly nonsense."

The story uses two different types of nonsense that we have encountered before. First, there is a nonsense world inhabited by sentient consonants and vowels. Then, that world is attacked by a second type of nonsense—unintelligible mock writing. Hence, the story envisions nonsense both as a creative force that builds worlds and a chaotic force that destroys worlds. The Turners' story brings both types of nonsense together to impart a spiritual lesson about prejudice.

Dr. Seuss's *On Beyond Zebra* is an abecedary of twenty nonsense letters that go beyond the letters of the regular alphabet. The book also evokes the cross-dimensional associations of nonsense. The additional nonsense letters are apparently needed to describe things experienced in another state of existence. One character explains,

> In the places I go there are things that I see
> That I never could spell if I stopped with the Z.
> I'm telling you this cause you're one of my friends.
> My alphabet starts where your alphabet ends.

Here again, an abecedarian formula harmonizes nonsense, entertainment, and spiritual experiences. We should put aside the notion that spirituality precludes or supersedes nonsense and entertainment. Furthermore, it is perfectly possible to restore the old spiritual and consciousness-raising uses of abecedaries.

An exercise in my course guided students as they wrote their own nonsense abecedaries. Students were asked to introspect and write about the personal feelings and experiences of composing an abecedary. The majority of students reported fascinating effects on their consciousness. Numerous students compared the exercise to a spiritual practice or mental discipline. Many said that the exercise inspired creativity or opened a hidden channel of the mind.

We live in a hurried world of instant gratification, and writing an abecedary is a time-consuming process that requires application. Even so, most students commented that they benefited from the exercise. Composing an abecedary can be a worthwhile project. You might well benefit from it, especially if you are interested in creative writing.

* * * *

Nonsense appears in scriptures and holy writings of various religions. The Yoga Vasistha is a compendium of Hindu sacred writings. This ancient holy text includes enigmatic stories such as "The Story of the Three Non-Existent Princes." Four types of nonsense that we discussed previously are discernable in this story:

> Once upon a time in a city which did not exist, there were three princes who were brave and happy. Of them two were unborn and the third had not been conceived. Unfortunately all their relatives died. The princes left their native city to go elsewhere.

During their journey the sun was very hot, and the three princes found shade under three trees: "Two did not exist and the third had not even been planted." They also discovered three rivers: "Two were dry and in the third there was no water. The princes had a refreshing bath and quenched their thirst in them." They eventually reached a city that had three beautiful palaces: "Two had not been built at all, and the third had no walls." The princes cooked rice and gave it to three holy men: "Two had no body and the third had no mouth." The princes then ate the remainder of the food. "They were greatly pleased. Thus they lived in that city for a long, long time in peace and joy."[54]

This story exemplifies erasure. G. C. Lichtenberg, the German physicist and satirist, created nonsense of this type and apparently discovered it independently. Then surrealist artists like Dali followed Lichtenberg's pattern to write their own original erasures. Erasure appeared independently in two different cultures thousands of years apart. Here is another case, then, that shows that patterns of nonsense are somehow inherent in language.

The Hindu story also contains an element of numerative nonsense, another type we also discussed previously. Specifically, "cooking 99 minus 100 grams of rice" uses number terms unintelligibly in a nonsensical recipe. Numerative nonsense also occurs in the Ramayana, a sacred epic of Hinduism. In one passage, for example, "He kept the five, obtained

---

54   *The Supreme Yoga*, 87.

the triad, took the triad, conquered the pair and then discarded the pair." Yet the work never establishes any context that would enable readers to determine what the number words are supposed to enumerate. Even so, the number terminology in the unintelligible passage somehow evokes a mysterious supernatural presence, and it does so without conveying definite coherent thoughts to the mind.

In overall structure, "The Story of the Three Non-Existent Princes" is a nonsensical travel narrative. Accordingly, we have now identified four types of nonsense that we discussed before in this one ancient Hindu story. Namely, we found erasure, numerative nonsense, a nonsensical recipe and a nonsensical travel narrative. That makes it plain that the typology of nonsense set out in chapter 3 is a useful instrument for analyzing and comprehending some holy texts.

The Bible begins with a series of self-contradictions and stunning reversals. Genesis creates a compelling story of Creation by directly contradicting itself multiple times. Specifically, in Genesis I plants existed before the sun and stars, while in Genesis II the sun and stars existed first, before plants. In Genesis I God created Adam and Eve together, but then in Genesis II God created Eve from Adam's rib. In fact, the whole account of Creation in Genesis is a mesmerizing crazy quilt of contradictory, conflicting, and inconsistent stories about what happened in the beginning.

According to modern scholars, the Creation story in Genesis is an amalgam of several earlier texts. Apparently the original compilers of the Bible treasured several separate traditional narratives about the Creation and wanted to preserve them despite their mutual inconsistencies. What gave the text of Genesis they compiled in that way its remarkable staying power, though?

The compelling power of Genesis's creation story is partly a function of its status in two major religions. However, some general rules regarding self-contradictions that we previously established on independent grounds also lend their impetus to the Creation story in Genesis. For instance, we saw that beginning a book with a brazen self-contradiction can be a highly effective means of getting readers' attention. We also saw that a series of nonsensical self-contradictions is the common structural formula behind several familiar playground rhymes. We saw that a nonsensical playground rhyme in that configuration can bring a vivid story to life in the mind, and we found that children chant those nonsensical playground rhymes together to forge social bonds. Similarly, self-contradictions are partly responsible for the enduring majesty of the Creation story told in Genesis. The Bible's many self-contradictions contribute to its unique tone of deep supernatural mystery.

"The Story of the Three Non-Existent Princes" and Genesis's story of Creation show that nonsense sometimes occurs in religious scriptures. No doubt other cases can be found, but these two cases are enough to establish the general point. They also demonstrate that the typology of nonsense opens a new level of rational analysis for comprehending some important religious texts.

Nonsense was once thought to project magical powers. Nonsense is directly connected to the supernatural through the practice of magic. In fact, ancient magicians thought they could alter reality by uttering just the right combinations of nonsense words. They uttered formulaic nonsense words for changing one thing into another, making things appear or disappear, or invoking supernatural beings. Magicians used specific formulas of nonsense prescribed for healing the sick, curing infertility, ensuring good luck, casting spells, defending themselves, and putting curses on enemies. Magicians and almost everyone else shared the belief that mysterious-sounding nonsense words wielded supernatural power.

Nonsense words that could supposedly transform reality by magic have a similar mysterious and exotic sound and appearance in various times and climes. To seem obscure and incomprehensible to everyone, magical nonsense must not resemble any known, familiar languages. Nonsense that supposedly causes magical changes should sound and look foreign to everyone who hears or reads it.

The Greek Magical Papyri are a collection of texts on scrolls that are about two thousand years old. They were discovered in the nineteenth century in the deserts of Egypt. These magical texts consist of incantations, chants, and rituals for attracting love, contacting superior beings, summoning spirits, attaining one's wishes, and the like. The magical texts were written in Greek following Alexander the Great's conquest of Egypt. They were recipes and procedures people used in magical rituals as part of their Greek folk religion. They are also a treasure trove of strange-sounding nonsense that was uttered expressly for various magical purposes.

In the texts, instructions for setting the stage and preparing for the magical procedure are written in Greek. Then, to make the magic happen, the seeker had to utter specific strange-sounding meaningless nonsense words in a specific combination, such as "naine basanaptatou eaptou menophaesme" and "araouazar bamesen kriphi niptoumi."

Such words and phrases are not part of any known language, and they make no intelligible sense at all to anyone, yet they impressed people as magic, probably in part because they were meaningless nonsense and sounded strange. Most people were persuaded that unintelligible nonsense emitted paranormal powers.

The occult scholar Émile Grillot de Givry collected some magical nonsense words from the Middle Ages. De Givry emphasized that people used to take magical nonsense words very seriously; an example from his *Illustrated Anthology of Sorcery, Magic and Alchemy* contains this passage:

> Tavar alcilo Sedoan acheir,
> Nestabo cacay extabor erional,
> Anapheta Dinotor Drion Sarao.[55]

---

55 Émile Grillot de Givry, *An Illustrated Anthology of Sorcery, Magic and Alchemy* (Causeway Books, 1973), 109.

Two miracle plays of the thirteenth century featured strange-sounding magical nonsense. In a miracle play by Ruteboeuf, the sorcerer, Salatin, conjured up the Devil. To do so, the sorcerer uttered bizarre words not belonging to any known language:

> Bagabi laca bachabé
> Lamac cahi achababé

Almost four centuries later, Rembrandt pictured the same bizarre style of magical nonsense language in his "Dr. Faustus" etching, which is inscribed with the strange words "adam te dageram" and "Amrtet algar algastna." Such magic words mean nothing and convey no coherent ideas to the mind, yet they are impressive and awe-inspiring because of their dark and mysterious foreign sound and appearance.

Magical nonsense words were sometimes inscribed in certain geometrical arrangements, such as word squares. Magical word squares were known as sacred grids. For example, repetitively uttering the nonsensical words arranged in the figure below was a spell for magical flying.

> ROLOR
> OBUFO
> LUAUL
> OFUBO
> ROLOR

In medieval Europe people uttered prescribed formulaic nonsense for healing various ailments. For instance, repeating the magical nonsense words "argidam, magidam, sturgidam" three times supposedly cured a toothache. Repeating the nonsense words "adam, bedem, alam, betur, alem, botem" nine times was a popular magical remedy for gastrointestinal disorders.

Nonsensical magical nonsense words often produce their uncanny effects by what is known as reduplication. Words like "ping-pong," "King Kong," "flip-flop," "knick-knack," "hocus-pocus," and "mumbo-jumbo" are reduplicatives. Reduplicatives have an engaging word rhythm that can produce a sense of deep supernatural mystery.

Adults may not always believe that odd-sounding nonsense chants can magically alter reality. However, the idea is still alive in popular children's literature. For example, Andrew Clements' book *Double Trouble in Walla Walla* ascribes magical powers to nonsense chants composed entirely of reduplicatives.

In the book, a little girl named Lulu got stuck uttering only reduplicatives. As a result, she inadvertently "opened up a knock 'em, sock 'em, wibble-wobble word warp." Lulu's strange affliction proved contagious, and soon everyone in her grammar school spoke reduplicative words uncontrollably. The school nurse mended Walla Walla reality by telling everyone to say all the reduplicatives they could think of at once. Together, the students uttered the following nonsensical chant of reduplicatives to close the word warp:

Ticky-tacky
Knick-knack
Koochie-koochie-koo!
Hubba-hubba
Rodger-dodger
Ooey-gooey-goo!
Hugger-mugger
Hob-nob
Pit-a-patter, bon-bon!
Wishy-washy
Squish-squash
Handy-dandy
Mish-mosh!

Funny-sounding and odd-looking words such as reduplicatives produce a peculiar effect on the mind that is somehow suggestive of magic. The Fairy Godmother in Walt Disney's animated film *Cinderella* said the reduplicative nonsense words "Wallaka-ballaka, nallaka-wallaka, bippidi-boppidi-boo" to cast a magical spell.

"The Witch Doctor," a popular song of the mid-1950s, gradually became a standard song for children. In the song, a lovesick man went to a witch doctor for help. The witch doctor taught his lovelorn client a magical chant of nonsensical reduplicatives to cast a spell on his girlfriend.

Zen Buddhism's koans are mental exercises that pose unanswerable nonsense questions as a path to enlightenment. Unintelligible questions like "What is the sound of one hand clapping?" put the mind in overdrive, which is what we would expect from our prior discussion of the mental effects of nonsense questions.

A Zen master takes each individual student's propensities and needs into account when assigning a particular koan to that student. The student must repeat the koan ceaselessly and become absorbed in it, even though the koan is a nonsense question that is beyond the capacity of logic and rational intellect.

Ultimately, the process drives the student to despair of ever attaining enlightenment by logical reasoning alone. The sudden illumination supposedly awakens the mind to a spiritual reality that transcends logic. The koan "What did your face look like before your mother and father were born?" uses nonsense to confront students with deep spiritual questions of personal identity. Koans show that nonsense questions can be a powerful instrument for consciousness-raising and spiritual transformation.

Glossolalia, or speaking in unknown tongues, uses meaningless, unintelligible nonsense to induce a state of ecstasy. Early Christians sometimes would spontaneously break out into a bout of glossolalia. Some Christians still practice glossolalia and surround it with a loose system of religious doctrines, Bible quotations, and folklore.

Believers maintain that talking in unknown tongues is a supernatural event in which the Holy Ghost talks to God through them. They believe that glossolalia is a more perfect form of language than human speech. They also say that glossolalia is the purest form of prayer.

Supposedly God understands glossolalia perfectly, but the unintelligible speech leaves Satan mystified. Therefore, believers talk in unknown tongues to God so that Satan will not overhear what they are saying.

Some believers talk in unknown tongues as a protective charm. I once saw a Christian high-wire walker who spoke in unknown tongues for self-protection. I watched him on television as he jabbered away meaninglessly while walking on a cable that stretched from a church steeple to the rooftop of a nearby building.

Analysis by linguists shows that glossolalia is a haphazard mixture of nonsense syllables from the speaker's native language. Believers hold that glossolalia is an actual, but unknown, language. Hence, talking in unknown tongues meets our criteria for a mock language.

Talking in unknown tongues does not require being religious or attending a church service. An ecstatic experience is not needed to start talking in unknown tongues. What is required is letting go of inhibitions. However, prolonging the nonsensical speech eventually does bring on a fascinating state of ecstasy. I know because I once jabbered myself into a truly amazing state of consciousness by talking in unknown tongues.

This kind of analysis opens the way for a novel comparative method of investigating transcendent consciousness.

Psychologists and neuroscientists face great difficulties in studying spiritual and transcendent states of consciousness. Consciousness is a private experience while science requires repeatable experiments that are testable by independent observers. Our structural principle of nonsenses may make it possible to distinguish between different states of spiritual consciousness.

We saw that various spiritual practices make use of nonsense of various types to induce various changes in conscious experience. Our structural principle says that each type of nonsense follows some rules and breaks others in its own distinctive combination. Glossolalia and koans are spiritual practices that use nonsense to raise consciousness. Glossolalia, you will recall, follows phonetic rules by selecting nonsense syllables from the speaker's own language. Meanwhile, the speaker shuns grammatical rules and must avoid meaningful combinations of nonsense syllables. That is an impressive mental balancing act, and it is no wonder that glossolalia induces states of ecstasy.

Koans, by contrast, generally respect the grammatical rules of language. Koans are also made up of meaningful words and they are usually interrogatives. The trouble with koans is that the words are not combined in ways that make sense; koans do not ask intelligible questions. A student who applies reason assiduously and relentlessly to such nonsense questions is eventually lifted into a transcendent cognitive state beyond logic.

Here are two different spiritual practices using nonsense. They can be differentiated by referring to their distinctive patterns of rule following and rule breaking. That, in turn, can serve as an independent standard for comparing different states of spiritual consciousness. Glossolalia produces a particular state of spiritual consciousness. Koans presumably produce a different particular state of spiritual consciousness. People's personal descriptions of the experiences of glossolalia and koans can be compared and correlated with corresponding differences in following rules and breaking rules. Perhaps these differences can also be correlated with differences in brain activity as revealed by CAT scans and nuclear magnetic resonance imagers.

Nonsense is often used for putting indescribable, seemingly transcendent experiences into words. If we are to believe mystics, ordinary language is unsuitable for describing transcendent consciousness. The English philosopher A. J. Ayer says, "If a mystic admits that the object of his vision is something which cannot be described, then he must also admit that he is bound to talk nonsense when he describes it."[56]

Mystical experiences are said to be ineffable, or indescribable. Mystics say that there is a profound disconnect between ordinary language and transcendent experiences. When mystics try to put their experiences into words, they say, "I just

56   Ayer, "God-Talk Is Evidently Nonsense," 144–145.

can't describe it" or "There are no words to describe it" or "It is impossible to describe this experience."

Ineffability was the primary characteristic American psychologist William James used to define mystical experiences. William James was right; ineffability is a striking characteristic of mystical consciousness. Anyone who has listened to people talk about their transcendent experiences would be familiar with phrases like "I can't describe it" and "impossible to describe."

How do these phrases function in mystics' accounts of their transcendent experiences? We need to know that detail since ineffability is a core defining characteristic of mystical consciousness. After all, mystics' words about their experiences are our sole source for comprehending ineffable mystical consciousness.

Saying that one's mystical experience is ineffable affects everything else the speaker might subsequently say about that experience. That is, saying that one's experience is ineffable establishes a special context for listeners' reception of the rest of the speaker's words. Specifically, it appears that we are not supposed to take the speaker's other words about the experience in their ordinary literal meanings.

William James noted that starkly self-contradictory expressions are common in the writings of eminent mystics. As examples, he cited "dazzling obscurity," "whispering silence," "the Soundless Sound," and "the teeming desert."[57] Self-

---

57   James, *The Varieties of Religious Experience*, 420–421.

contradictions like these seem to somehow correspond to a universal mystical intuition of a transcendent unity underlying all things.

Self-contradictions are not the only type of nonsense that people use as they try to find words for expressing their profound transcendent experiences. In a later chapter, we will analyze some different patterns of nonsense that people talk when they try to recount other kinds of transcendent experiences. That will be further proof that rational principles of nonsense are a useful adjunct to ordinary logical principles for thinking about transcendent experiences.

Nonsense purportedly figures into some core religious ideas and beliefs. In *Language, Truth, and Logic*, A. J. Ayer writes that "all utterances about the nature of God are nonsensical...If the assertion that there is a god is nonsensical, then the atheist's assertion that there is no god is equally nonsensical."[58]

Logical positivists thought of nonsense as a defect of language. Hence, they were dismissive of religious ideas by deeming them nonsense. However, we now realize that nonsense is a good thing, for the most part. Furthermore, nonsense is a more complex order of language that supervenes on ordinary language. Could nonsense language sometimes be better at expressing religious ideas than ordinary language is?

Certain familiar religious ideas plainly resemble types of nonsense we previously identified. For instance, according

---

58 Quoted in Jack Huberman, *The Quotable Atheist* (New York, NY: Nation Books, 2007), 20–21.

to the Christian doctrine of the Trinity, God, Jesus, and the Holy Ghost are one single being. How can one single entity be three distinct entities at the same time? In fact, the notion of the Trinity appears to satisfy our established definition of numerative nonsense.

The line between spiritual doctrine and spiritual practice can sometimes be hard to draw. In the medieval period, people sometimes contemplated the Trinity as a logico-spiritual exercise. They felt that pondering the Trinity gave them insight into the identity and nature of God. Pondering the numerical nonsense of the Trinity was then a spiritual practice for inducing transcendent consciousness. In that respect, then, the Trinity is comparable to glossolalia and koans. Accordingly, the method of studying transcendent consciousness described earlier in the chapter might also apply to the Trinity. We could then compare the various states of spiritual consciousness produced by glossolalia, koans, and contemplating the Trinity.

. . . .

Nonsense is an illuminating metaphor for life itself. What is the meaning of life? Does life have a meaning at all? Is life itself, and the entire cosmos that houses it, meaningless nonsense? Big questions like those have fueled religious and philosophical debates for centuries.

In the aftermath of World War I, some brilliant European thinkers and writers took an extreme position on the big question of human existence. The absurdists, as they were known, maintained that the universe, together with everything in it, including human existence, is meaningless and nonsensical. Alfred Jarry, Albert Camus, and Samuel Beckett, the best-known absurdists, wrote thought-provoking and entertaining literary nonsense. Their works resonated with millions of people who were traumatized by war and could therefore more easily accept that life might be meaningless and unintelligible. In the war, nonsense had intruded itself into people's lives and somehow needed to be taken into account. As G. K. Chesterton put it:

> If nonsense is really to be the literature of the future, it must have its own version of the Cosmos to offer; the world must not only be tragic, romantic, and religious, it must be nonsensical also.[59]

Absurdism was a literary movement rather than a clearly articulated philosophical position. Absurdist ideas were too nebulous to be put together into a single coherent system of thought. Hence, like some other grand theories of everything, absurdism grew so large that it fell in under its own weight. Specifically, the following reasoning shows how that happened.

Absurdism is the doctrine that the universe, and its entire contents, including even human life itself, is meaningless and unintelligible. Now, absurdism is obviously something that exists in the universe. Therefore, absurdism itself is meaningless and unintelligible nonsense.

---

59   Huberman, *The Quotable Atheist*, 9.

Furthermore, something can be meaningless and unintelligible only against a general background in which some other things are meaningful and intelligible. For instance, consider the sentence "There is a smomastrum of snanage dancing tender equations within the bionic stratosphere." We can say with complete confidence that the sentence is deliberate, meaningless, unintelligible nonsense. However, we can say that only because we can contrast the sentence with so many other sentences that are meaningful and that do make sense. In other words, if there were no meaningful, intelligible things in the universe, then there could be no meaningless, unintelligible nonsense either. For unintelligible nonsense to exist, there must be some meaningful, intelligible thing with which to contrast it.

Absurdism went too far, therefore, in proclaiming that absolutely everything in the universe is nonsensical. Even so, nonsense is a compelling and persuasive metaphor for all of existence, and human life in particular. The universe we live in is so vast that we cannot clearly understand what size or shape it might be, or even whether it is finite in extension. And, like nonsense, many things in life are sometimes confusing. The perplexity we feel in struggling with life's dilemmas is comparable to reading a work of deliberate nonsense.

In sum, nonsense is a primordial element of spiritual and religious thought, writing, experience, and practice. Hence, the sense of nonsense has a spiritual dimension in addition to a psychological dimension. Nonsense permeates the spiritual life, from abecedaries and other holy texts to con-sciousness-raising practices such as koans, glossolalia, and meditating on the Trinity. Plainly, unintelligible nonsense can sometimes be a more effective linguistic vehicle for spiritual thought than intelligible, literal language can.

Accordingly, although absurdism was an incoherent and self-defeating doctrine, it still propounded an insightful and provocative metaphor. Life itself, one might say, is a kind of nonsense tale.

.

Chapter 6

NONSENSE AND KNOWLEDGE

Nonsense is the end result of all sense.

Georges Bataille

Nonsense interacts dynamically with reason in the quest for knowledge. To talk about nonsense and rational knowledge in the same breath seems contrary to common sense, for reason and nonsense supposedly directly oppose each other. In this case, however, common sense is a vast oversimplification. And in reality, the concept of nonsense is as indispensable for rigorous rational inquiry as are the concepts of truth and falsehood. This chapter will present and support six statements about relationships between nonsense and knowledge. Together, they paint a more accurate, complex, interesting, and colorful picture of nonsense in the search for rational knowledge than common sense does.

Nonsense Is Neither True Nor False

Many people assume that nonsense is the same as falsehood or that nonsense is a particularly blatant and glaring form of falsehood. Hence, the statement that nonsense is neither true nor false may seem counterintuitive at first. Nonsense and falsehood move in separate planes of thought and analysis. Confusing them causes no immediate harmful effect on the mind. Down the line, however, confusing nonsense with falsehood severely compromises one's ability to think cogently about some important questions of science, psychology, religion, and spirituality.

Falsehood is the opposite of truth. Nonsense is the opposite of meaningful, intelligible language. Hence, since the two concepts do not have the same opposite, nonsense and falsehood are not the same. Accordingly, if nonsense and falsehood are confused, much nonsense, falsehood, and confusion will result.

Historically, concepts of nonsense, truth, and falsehood were discovered in that order. Ancient shamans and magicians understood that nonsense is a meaningless, unintelligible form of language that projected special powers. Before there was a clear formal concept of truth or falsehood, Heraclitus scorned nonsense as meaningless and unintelligible, using it as a term of reproach. Parmenides, the father of deductive logic, propounded the concept of truth, or that which is the case independently of anyone's opinion. Then, decades later, Plato defined the notion of falsehood, or that which is not the case independently of anyone's opinion, as the opposite of truth. Seeing that the concept of nonsense came first, truth second, and falsehood third makes it plain that nonsense and falsehood are not the same.

Statements Are Either True or False, and Typically They Are Declarative Sentences of Literal Meaning

Knowing the literal meaning of a statement is necessary for determining whether it is true or false. For example, consider the statement "Some dogs are brown." Anyone who knows the literal meaning of that statement and has a modicum of experience observing dogs would know that the statement is true.

Next, consider the statement "A bat is a kind of bird." Anyone who knows the literal meaning of that statement and has a modicum of experience observing bats would agree that the statement is false. Evidently, then, knowing the literal meaning of a statement is necessary for determining whether the statement is true or false. In other words, "true" and "false" are terms that apply specifically to literal, meaningful statements.

Now, consider the sentence "A plurgish gloapster startled a whining, illiterate rainbow." This is a grammatically correct sentence, and it is meaningless, unintelligible nonsense. Because the sentence has no intelligible meaning, the question of its being true or false simply does not arise.

Asking whether the nonsensical declarative sentence above is true or false is like asking whether a pumpkin pie is awake or asleep, or whether the square root of a number is pink or yellow. The distinction between truth and falsehood simply does not apply to nonsensical declarative sentences.

A declarative sentence must be meaningful and intelligible to be a true or false statement. In other words, unintelligibility is a prerequisite for applying the distinction between truth and falsehood. Therefore, nonsensical, unintelligible declarative sentences are neither true nor false.

Deliberate nonsense sentences like "A plurgish gloapster startled a whining, illiterate rainbow" are not likely to be mistaken for a meaningful statement. In cases like that, therefore, confusing nonsense with falsehood does not present a problem. Sometimes, however, a sentence that is actually unintelligible nonsense may look to someone like a meaningful, intelligible true-or-false statement. Then, when that person tries to apply ordinary logic to the disguised nonsense sentence, particularly baffling problems arise.

Later on, we will see that precisely that kind of problem has arisen in the history of the quest for knowledge. The distinction between nonsense and falsehood is an important principle of reason. Nonsense and falsehood are concepts that belong to two different levels of rational analysis.

Nonsense Comes In Degrees

Zeno was the first philosopher to observe that one thing can be more nonsensical and unintelligible than some other unintelligible, nonsensical things. Specifically, Zeno said that common-sense assumptions about motion actually lead to more nonsensical consequences than does Parmenides's position that reality is stationary, timeless and unitary. Zeno's insight was that unintelligibility lies in a continuum, or a spectrum of shades and degrees.

I wrote the two pairs of sentences below to illustrate Zeno's point. Each of the sentences is equal in length. Yet, in each pair, the second sentence is plainly more nonsensical and unintelligible than the first sentence:

> Five silly cleebers solemnly climbed up a nurgly spiral staircase.
> Five flispy blargers toobled some spimsy, flurgish spergwhallers into drukes.

> The mystic monkey chattered and threw equations at the spectators.
> The lonely, vibrating percentage sang religious carrots and venerable rails.

The degrees of nonsense and unintelligibility that we perceive in comparing sentences like those above can be roughly quantified. Hence, in general, the greater the percentage of made-up meaningless words in a sentence of near-English, the more nonsensical the sentence becomes. Similarly, in general, the greater the number of incommensurable things and attributes that a sentence of categorical nonsense mismatches, the more nonsensical the sentence becomes.

Examples could also be written that would illustrate Zeno's point for almost any type of nonsense that we have named. In other words, numerative nonsense, conjunctive nonsense, nonsense stories, mock languages—these and many other types—all can be created in varying degrees of unintelligibility. Nonsense syllables, for one, are an exception; making nonsense syllables that would be more nonsensical and unintelligible than others is a difficult task to contemplate. The rare exception proves the rule, though, and nonsense of most types conforms to Zeno's precept.

Lewis Carroll touched on the notion of shades and degrees of nonsense. In *Through the Looking-Glass*, Alice encountered the disputatious Red Queen. The Queen's conversation went on as follows:

> "When you say 'hill,'" the Queen interrupted, "I could show you hills, in comparison with which you'd call that a valley."
>
> "No, I shouldn't," said Alice, surprised into contradicting her at last; "a hill can't be a valley, you know. That would be nonsense—"
>
> The Red Queen shook her head. "You may call it 'nonsense' if you like," she said, "but I've heard nonsense, compared with which that would be as sensible as a dictionary!"[60]

---

60 Carroll, *Through the Looking-Glass*, 46.

Sir Arthur Eddington, a great astronomer and physicist of the twentieth century, discussed what he dubbed the physicists' "problem of nonsense." Eddington granted that it may be nonsense for physicists to assert that realities exist beyond the laws of physics. Yet, Eddington added, it is even more nonsensical for physicists to deny that such realities exist. According to Eddington, then, the weighing and comparing of different shades of and degrees of nonsense does have a place in science.

Nonsense Sometimes Comes True

Nonsense is neither true nor false, but new truths emerge from it. Sentences that would be unintelligible nonsense in one era might be intelligible, and even true, in a different era. For example, consider the sentence "All four of John's grandparents perished in a ship that sank long before his mother or father were born."

In 1900 this sentence would have been considered unintelligible nonsense. Then came discoveries such as DNA, mapping the human genome, genetic engineering, cloning and technology for retrieving objects from shipwrecks deep beneath the sea. Nowadays, therefore, the situation presented in the sentence is intelligible, and reproductive biotechnology might someday even make a sentence like that true. Since 1910 new knowledge has been discovered of connections in nature that turned a previously nonsensical sentence into a meaningful, intelligible sentence.

Consider the sentence "Two men got married to each other at city hall today." Again, in 1900 in the United States, this sentence would have been unintelligible nonsense. In fact, I specifically remember similar sentences being used as examples of self-contradictory nonsense in graduate philosophy seminars in the mid-1960s. Then came the gay rights movement and court cases and changes in Americans' attitudes toward homosexuality. Nowadays, therefore, the sentence is intelligible, and sentences like that are true in cities in the United States every day.

Galileo's claim that Earth circled the sun along with Venus, Mars, and Jupiter seemed not false but unintelligible to most people in his time. Galileo's claim implied that Earth is one of the heavenly bodies, like Venus and Jupiter, but that was unintelligible nonsense because Earth is clearly down here!

In other words, nonsense is not necessarily a permanent state. The apparent meaninglessness and unintelligibility of a sentence may be a function of changeable external circumstances, such as a lack of knowledge. The principle that nonsense comes in degrees helps us comprehend some cases of nonsense's transmutation into truth.

Ancient alchemy was the forerunner of today's science of chemistry. Alchemy arose in the Hellenistic period when Greek philosophy, with its rational principles, encountered traditional Egyptian technologies for making materials. Early alchemists took it for granted that strange-sounding, meaningless, unintelligible words could emanate magical powers.

They were nonsensical magical words like we considered in the previous chapter. Alchemists were looking for just the right combinations of nonsensical magic words to set mysterious forces into motion. Supposedly those mystical forces would somehow interact with the physical materials used in an alchemical procedure. The purpose of uttering the nonsensical formulas over the physical materials was to transmute less desirable substances into more desirable ones.

Numerative nonsense—unintelligible, meaningless language modeled on numbers and mathematical terminology—also appears in some early alchemical writings. Strangely evocative formulas like "the five overcomes the three" occur in writings by alchemists, yet the writings contain no clue as to what the number words supposedly enumerate. The alchemists' words do not convey coherent thoughts to the mind.

In alchemy, then, multiple types of nonsense ran in tandem with observable physical processes. Occasionally an alchemist would stumble onto a useful discovery, and gradually alchemists learned more and more about material substances and chemical reactions. Then, in the sixteenth century, Paracelsus said that alchemists should pursue the practical goal of making medicines rather than trying fruitlessly to make gold. In the seventeenth century, Robert Boyle wrote *The Skeptical Chymist*. Although it is somewhat ambiguous and vague by today's standards, Boyle's book is largely intelligible. In the eighteenth century, Lavoisier gave the science a mathematical language and a sound experimental basic in his

Elements of Chemistry. When reading ancient alchemical writings, Paracelsus, Boyle, and Lavoisier in sequence, alchemical, magical, and numerative nonsense seems gradually to morph into intelligible scientific truth. Nonsense gradually transmuted into intelligible truth by degrees over the many years of chemistry's history.

Nonsense May Be Implicated in Some Basic Concepts of Science

Science seems to tolerate nonsense better than theory would indicate. In science nonsense is a strongly negative quantity. After all, science signifies reason and truth, while nonsense is a hallmark of irrationality. Paradoxically, though, science has put up with a seemingly unintelligible concept of time for many centuries.

Some scientists have concluded that an essential aspect of the conventional concept of time is unintelligible nonsense. For example, reflective of early twenty-first-century scientific thinking, in *New Scientist* Marcus Chown has said,

> At super-high energies, like those believed to have occurred in the earliest moments of the big bang, time loses all meaning.

Science writer Amanda Gefter has stated,

> This, of course, raises the question of what came before the big bang and how long it lasted. Unfortunately, at this point basic ideas begin to fail us; the concept "before" becomes meaningless. In the words of Stephen

Hawking, it's like asking for directions to a place north
of the North Pole.

And they contrast sharply with Isaac Newton's words in
stating his theory of classical mechanics, that "absolute, true
and mathematical time, of itself, and from its own nature,
flows equably without relation to anything external."

Newton's physics was the crowning achievement of science and the epitome of reason from the seventeenth through
nineteenth centuries, yet the notion of the flow of time
enshrined in Newton's classical mechanics is unintelligible
nonsense from the standpoint of twenty-first-century physics. Here we see again how what is thought of as intelligible
or unintelligible may shift dramatically as science acquires
new knowledge.

The more things change, though, the more they stay the
same. Some ancient Greek philosophers questioned whether
time is intelligible, and the question has been debated inter-
mittently ever since. "What came before the big bang?" has
a previous incarnation in "What was God doing before he
created the universe?"

St. Augustine replied that the question itself is meaningless nonsense, arguing that God brought time into being at
the Creation, along with everything else. Accordingly, since
time began at the Creation, to ask what happened before the
Creation is unintelligible.

St. Augustine faced the same objection from rival philosophers in his era. They insisted that time is infinite, with

no beginning and no end, hence that there obviously was a time before God created the world. Debates about the intelligibility of time seem to be an enduring theme of organized rational knowledge, including science.

Scientists generally acknowledge that there is a major problem concerning nonsense at the very center of twenty-first-century physics. Namely, physics' two most successful theories generate nonsense when they are combined. Furthermore, the problem is widely known, and scientists put up with the astonishing paradox as a matter of course, as described in 2013 by Jacob Aron in *New Scientist*:

> Our two best theories for describing reality are quantum mechanics and general relativity. So far, however, attempts to combine the equations in these disparate theories have produced nonsensical answers.

In sum, an element of nonsense seems to be tolerated in science as a practical matter. Ideological principles that would seemingly exclude nonsense entirely from science are suspended. Apparently, science has no choice but to abide some amount of nonsense, even in basic concepts such as time.

Nonsense Sometimes Serves as a Placeholder in the Search for Rational Knowledge

A singer who forgets some of the words of a song may fill in the gap with improvised nonsense syllables and rescue the performance. Similarly, scientists sometimes fill in gaps in scientific knowledge with nonsense, even knowing that it is nonsense, as a temporary stand-in for truth. For instance, unintelligible nonsense is produced by combining the equations of quantum mechanics with the equations of general relativity. However, the nonsense is tolerated for the sake of the enormous amounts of knowledge the two theories produce separately. I dub this kind of situation "placeholder nonsense."

Placeholder nonsense holds a place open in language and mind, in lieu of secure knowledge concerning a subject. Nonsense is put in as a placeholder, anticipating that someday it may be replaced by confirmed truth and sound knowledge. In that respect then, placeholder nonsense is an aspirational form of thought and language looking forward toward eventual new truth. Martin Gardner described how Arthur Eddington attributed that very status to nonsense in physics.

"Jabberwocky" was a favorite of the British astronomer Arthur Stanley Eddington and is alluded to several times in his writings. In *New Pathways in Science*, he likens the abstract syntactical structure of the poem to that modern branch of mathematics known as group theory. In *The Nature of the Physical World*, he points out that the physicist's description of

an elementary particle is really a kind of "Jabberwocky"—
words applied to "something unknown" that is "doing what
we don't know what." Because the description contains numbers, science is able to impose a certain amount of order on
the phenomena and make successful predictions about them.
Eddington wrote:

> By contemplating eight circulating electrons in one atom
> and seven circulating electrons in another, we begin to
> realize the difference between oxygen and nitrogen.
> Eight slithy toves gyre and gimble in the oxygen wabe;
> seven in nitrogen. By admitting a few numbers, even
> "Jabberwocky" may become scientific. We can now ven-
> ture on a prediction; if one of its toves escapes, oxy-
> gen will be masquerading in a garb properly belonging
> to nitrogen. In the stars and nebulae, we do find such
> wolves in sheep's clothing, which might otherwise have
> startled us. It would not be a bad reminder of the essen-
> tial unknownness of the fundamental entities of physics
> to translate it into "Jabberwocky"; provided all num-
> bers—all metrical attributes—are unchanged, it does
> not suffer in the least.[61]

Nonsense also apparently functioned as a placeholder for
Francis Galton as he wrestled with solving problems in his
mind. Galton (1822–1911) was an influential scientist who
contributed to fields as diverse as meteorology, geography,
genetics, statistics, and psychology. He also invented identifi-
cation by fingerprints.

---

61 Carroll and Gardner, *The Annotated Alice*, 192–193.

Galton was habitually introspective. He paid close attention to his inner process of thinking about problems. Galton said that he never thought in ordinary words. Sometimes, though, he would experience an accompaniment of nonsense words in his mind as he was deep in thought, working at solving problems. He said that experiencing the nonsense words was just "as the notes of a song might accompany thought."[62]

. . . .

To summarize, nonsense is an integral factor in reason and the pursuit of truth. Nonsense is neither true nor false, yet nonsense comes in degrees and sometimes transmutes into new truths. Nonsense seems to be built into some basic concepts of science, such as time, and therefore nonsense serves as a placeholder in the search for knowledge.

Nonsense interacts dynamically with reason in the quest for knowledge, and we have developed a body of systematic knowledge about nonsense itself. Can we apply rational knowledge about nonsense to speed up the process of acquiring knowledge alone or point it in promising new directions? Those are questions for the future. In the meantime, we will look at some implications and applications of the rational principles of nonsense developed thus far.

---

62   Galton, "Thought Without Words," 29.

THE THEORY OF NONSENSE

It's frustrating to know in your heart that what you've just heard is nonsense but not to be able to pinpoint why it is nonsense.

Robert J. Gula

Common sense is wrong about nonsense, for common sense views nonsense as an unknowable, formless nothingness that is inherently separate from reason and logic. However, in this book we have reduced a large amount of knowledge about nonsense to a few transparent statements that are rationally comprehensible and confirmable. In effect, the statements in this book form an emerging preliminary theory of nonsense. This chapter will shore up the theory by refining concepts, closing loopholes, and forestalling foreseeable objections.

Nonsense operates by its own intelligible, internal logic. Aristotelian logic works only with true or false statements that are of literal meaning. In other words, it is a binary code that allows only two values: true and false. Moreover, according to Aristotle's law of the excluded middle, a statement must be either true or false.

Earlier, though, we saw that nonsensical sentences are neither true nor false, even if they look like statements. Accordingly, then, we can think of nonsense as a third value of logic, apart from truth and falsehood. Yet, as we also saw, in some cases nonsense can somehow transmute into truth. Furthermore, nonsense exists and is defined in terms of the same rules and conventions that govern ordinary language and logic.

The upshot of all this is that rational principles of nonsense constitute an auxiliary non-Aristotelian logic of three values. In effect, a piece of reason was missing. By filling in the vacant space, the theory of nonsense opens a new level of reason and analysis.

Borderline Nonsense

Nonsense is bounded in part by borderline cases. Common sense puts nonsense on one side of an unbridgeable divide and meaningful language on the opposite side. The reality of the situation is not so simple, though. Some language falls somewhere in the middle and blurs the boundary between nonsense and meaningful language. As James Thurber said,

"Ours is a precarious language, as every writer knows, in which the merest shadow line often separates affirmation from negation, sense from nonsense, and one sex from the other."[63]

Reflecting on borderline cases brings the concept of nonsense into sharper focus. After all, borderline cases of nonsense exist because there are clear-cut cases of nonsense with which to contrast them.

Ornamental English

What is known as ornamental English provides illuminating borderline cases of nonsense. Ornamental English is a form of decorative writing used mainly in Japan. Using writing as a decoration is a time-honored tradition of Japan. In the aftermath of World War II, many Japanese favorably associated the English language with modernization. Strange messages, such as those below, soon began to appear on clothing and accessories manufactured for domestic consumption.

On a handbag:

> ReSpice Enjoy fashion life,
> Nice to Heart and Just Impression

On another handbag:

> The New York City Theater District
> Is where you can and us, anyone

---

63 Thurber, *Lanterns and Lances*, 62.

On an eyeglasses case:

> This case packs my dream and
> Eyeglasses

On a pencil case:

> Tenderness is completed a pastel

Throughout much of Asia, products that are labeled in English sell better. Since few who purchase the products can actually read English, the meaning, or lack thereof, does not matter. Hence, ornamental English is meant to be seen, not read. Somebody who speaks only English could not comprehend the bizarre messages of ornamental English. But is it nonsense?

Usually, ornamental English results from the literal translation of typically Japanese phrases and sentiments into English. In that sense, then, they are ragged translations. Theoretically, a skilled translator could recover the original Japanese thoughts and render them meaningfully into English.

On the other hand, the odd writing seen on Japanese products attracted attention in the West, and people attempted to reproduce it. To make a fashion statement, American and British designers began to adorn garments with strange messages similar to ornamental English. For instance, a British manufacturer emblazoned the incomprehensible words "Rodeo-100 Percent Boys for Atomic Atlas" on a fashionable jacket. Hence, ornamental English is a transitional phenomenon with one foot in meaningful language and the other foot in unintelligible nonsense.

Baby Talk

Baby talk, or motherese, is also midway between meaningful language and nonsense. Adults sometimes use simplified grammar and exaggerated intonation when talking to infants or toddlers. Some adults say that baby talk makes it easier for children to understand language. Some adults justify baby talk as an expression of affection.

Baby talk also contains a smattering of silly sounding, made-up nonsense expressions such as "kitchy-kitchy-coo." Mostly, however, baby talk is not nonsense, but meaningful language made more accessible to the young. In other words, for the most part, baby talk is simplified sense, not nonsense.

* * * *

In sum, ornamental English and baby talk straddle the fence between meaningful language and unintelligible nonsense. Additional forms of language can be found that are intermediary between sense and nonsense. However, it is important to remember that borderline cases do not imperil the concept of nonsense. To reiterate, borderline cases of nonsense exist because there are clear-cut cases of nonsense with which to contrast them.

Metalanguage

Nonsense can be described meaningfully in metalanguage, which is language about language. Does the theory of nonsense harbor the seeds of its own destruction? Some would say that there is a built-in paradox in the very notion of such a theory, for the theory consists of numerous declarative sentences that are purportedly about unintelligible nonsense. Specifically, the sentences supposedly describe, categorize, or analyze nonsense or its effects.

Now, presumably a declarative sentence must be either meaningful or else it is nonsense. But into which of these two categories should we put declarative sentences about nonsense? Are they meaningful or are they nonsense?

How could sentences like that be meaningful, though? If nonsense itself is meaningless, then how could declarative sentences about nonsense be meaningful? If they must be meaningless, however, rational inquiry into the subject would be impossible. The entire notion of a theory of nonsense would collapse into incoherence.

In other words, the apparent paradox threatens to invalidate the entire edifice of knowledge about nonsense that this book has constructed. But, fortunately, a concept known to logicians and philosophers as metalanguge can resolve the supposed paradox. Metalanguage is language that is about language. The sentences below will help explain the concept:

> Jack has four sisters.
> "Jack" has four letters.

Elephants are social animals.
"Elephants" is a plural noun.

The first and third sentences above are about things in extralinguistic reality. But, the second and fourth sentences are about language—specifically, the proper noun "Jack" and the general noun "elephants"—hence these sentences are examples of metalanguage. Placing the words "Jack" and "elephants" in quotation marks is a conventional way of indicating that the sentences are metalanguage.

Metalanguage can be about nonsense as easily as it can be about meaningful language. Metalanguage about nonsense can be meaningful even though the nonsense itself is meaningless. In other words, it is quite possible to talk intelligibly about nonsense, even though nonsense itself is unintelligible.

Now, the statements in this book that make up the theory of nonsense are instances of metalanguage. Furthermore, although nonsense itself is neither true nor false, this book's metalinguistic statements about nonsense are either true or false—mostly true, I believe; therefore, the existence of metalanguage, or language about language, makes a rational theory of nonsense possible.

Metalanguage also enables us to incorporate unintelligible nonsense within larger structures of meaningful language. A meaningful sentence can be made that surrounds a piece of nonsense and swallows it whole. For instance, quoting nonsense is one way of encasing it within a meaningful sentence. Consider the pair of sentences below:

Reluctant garbage jabbers in green.
Uncle Hamperd took a whiff of nitrous oxide and said,
    "Reluctant garbage jabbers in green."

The first sentence is unintelligible nonsense. Nevertheless, the second sentence, which directly quotes the first, is meaningful as a report of something somebody said. In other words, a sentence that directly quotes a nonsensical utterance may be meaningful. In summary, the concept of metalanguage resolves certain puzzles concerning the possibility of meaningful language about unintelligible nonsense.

Resolving Disputes Through Nonsense

Calling proposed new ideas "unintelligible nonsense" is a common form of objection in rational debates. Reasonable people sometimes disagree over whether proposed ideas are nonsense, yet there are no public rules and conventions, no rational standards for settling disagreements like those.

The theory of nonsense provides a sound rational basis for resolving some such disputes. Specifically, we saw that nonsense can be deliberate or involuntary. Either way, though, nonsense has the same structural patterns.

Now, presumably, scientists and academicians don't talk nonsense on purpose. If they lapse into unintelligible language and ideas, their nonsense is involuntary. Still, we can prove it is nonsense if its structural pattern matches one or more of the many types of deliberate nonsense we have already identified.

The principle seems obvious. However, a specific example is necessary. The following demonstration uses the typology of nonsense to resolve a documented historical dispute concerning unintelligibility. The specific dispute has to do with an ancient magical text known as the Emerald Tablet.

Apollonius of Tyana, an ancient holy man and wonder worker, supposedly discovered the work when he descended to the underworld. Apollonius claimed he had found a secret subterranean chamber in which an old man sat upon a golden throne. In his hand, the man held a tablet made of pure emerald. Apollonius saw an inscription on the tablet that he memorized and recorded for posterity. Apollonius attributed the inscription to Hermes Trismegistus, a renowned magician.

The Emerald Tablet kept eminent scholars and hobbyists busy for centuries trying to decipher its meaning. Many were convinced that it contained some deep secret of the universe or the key to unlimited wealth. For example, Sir Isaac Newton took the Emerald Tablet seriously, pondered its meaning, and translated it into English. Many other luminaries solemnly studied it, too, but the many interpretations that have been offered vary widely.

Other scholars characterized Apollonius as an impostor and charlatan and claimed that he made up the whole story. They said that the Emerald Tablet is a hoax, and that it is meaningless nonsense. Until now, however, there has not been a rational method for settling the dispute. Let us look at the text of the Emerald Tablet and see what the theory of nonsense can tell us.

The text is composed of cryptic sentences:

> The truth, certainty, truest, without untruth. What is above is like what is below. What is below is like what is above. The miracle of unity is to be attained. Everything is formed from the contemplation of unity, and all things come about from unity, by means of adaptation. Its parents are the Sun and Moon. It was borne by the wind and nurtured by the Earth. Every wonder is from it and its power is complete....This is the power of all strength—it overcomes that which is delicate and penetrates through solids. This was the means of the creation of the world. And in the future wonderful developments will be made, and this is the way. I am Hermes the Threefold Sage, so named because I hold the three elements of all the wisdom. And thus ends the revelation of the work of Sun.[64]

An analysis in terms of the typology of nonsense solves the riddle of the Emerald Tablet, for the text plainly consists of several types of nonsense that we already identified and described. Specifically, the text consists of elements of self-contradiction, numerative nonsense, figurative nonsense, nonreferential pronouns, and pseudo-profound nonsense.

In an exercise, my students discovered they could use the Emerald Tablet as an abstract pattern for making other works of nonsense that sound just as mysterious and profound.

---

64   Shah, *The Sufis*, 240–241.

For instance, an often-cited portion of the text is "What is above is like what is below. What is below is like what is above. The miracle of unity is to be attained." My students easily wrote sentences modeled on that pattern that sounded equally enigmatic and deep. For instance, one student wrote, "The within arises from the without and the without arises from the within—the manifestation of the Absolute." Another student wrote, "The odd embraces the even, and the even embraces the odd—the timeless process of Essence."

This analysis shows that in some cases a systematic typology of nonsense can be used to resolve disputes concerning unintelligibility. Even so, the method has three significant limitations. First, the method is effective for rational thinkers whose desire and interest are to seek truth. People who are fixated on an ideology are unlikely to be swayed if applying the method contradicts their cherished beliefs. For example, hobbyists who spend their lives trying to unlock a hidden meaning in the Emerald Tablet would probably be unmoved by the above analysis.

Second, the method won't work for all disputes concerning unintelligibility, for the method works by matching a disputed case to known structural patterns of deliberate nonsense. However, we have not identified and characterized all types of deliberate nonsense. Therefore, we cannot conclude that a disputed case is *not* nonsense, merely because we are unable to match it to a known structural pattern.

Third, we saw that calling a proposed idea unintelligible nonsense is generally regarded as a particularly powerful, even final, kind of objection. However, its power, efficacy, and finality have been greatly exaggerated, for even a clear, incontrovertible determination that a notion is unintelligible nonsense does not always invalidate the notion. In reality, proving that an idea is nonsense doesn't necessarily have the dire consequences that proponents of such objections imagine. Sometimes we accept an idea with grace and ease even if we know it is unintelligible.

Judges sometimes impose nonsensical sentences on perpetrators of particularly heinous crimes. A judge may sentence a condemned prisoner to "six consecutive life terms plus fifty-five years," for example. Sentences like that are plainly unintelligible nonsense.

Theoretically, if a judge handed down a sentence that was meaningless and unintelligible, the sentence should be invalid, for how could a prisoner be required to serve a nonsensical sentence? But what actually happens in cases like that? Defense attorneys don't protest. The legal system doesn't fall apart, and the court and penal system continue functioning as usual.

In the real world, nonsense is mostly harmless. Still, there are plenty of exceptions. Accordingly, the next chapter will discuss common misuses of nonsense.

Chapter 8

MISUSING NONSENSE

Nonsense draws evil after it.

C. S. Lewis

A few individuals misappropriate the powers of nonsense to manipulate others. The theory developed in this book makes it easier to recognize misuses of nonsense and to blunt their ill effects. This chapter will examine six common patterns or contexts of misusing nonsense. Specifically, nonsense has been used for imposture, bogus prophecies, totalitarian control, mock profundity, pseudoscientific theories, and self-deception.

Imposture

Impostors are colorful, charismatic figures who sometimes come to the attention of forensic psychiatrists and law enforcement officers. Impostors beguile others with fabricated tales of their supposed personal accomplishments and adventures. Impostors pretend to be intelligence agents, military heroes, royalty, or, in one case, a space shuttle pilot. Nonsense is one of impostors' favorite tools for fooling their gullible admirers.

In 1701 a blond, blue-eyed Frenchman who was only seventeen years old appeared in England. He identified himself as Psalmanazar, although nobody ever learned his real name. Psalmanazar told everyone he was a Christianized cannibal from the recently discovered island of Formosa. He ate raw meat and went around semi nude in public. Psalmanazar's fabricated descriptions of his supposed homeland held people spellbound, and he soon gathered a large following. In 1704 Psalmanazar published an illustrated book describing the customs, religion, and architecture of Formosa, and the book quickly became a major bestseller.

Psalmanazar told his enthralled audiences that Formosans sacrificed eighteen thousand male infants annually as a religious rite. He said that great herds of elephants and giraffes roamed his homeland. He claimed that Formosans lived to be a hundred years old and were rich in gold and silver.

To support the character he invented, Psalmanazar devised a meaningless mock language, complete with a nonsense alphabet, which he claimed was "Formosan." He made a prayer book and carried it as a prop. Inside were crude drawings of the sun, moon, and stars, together with passages written in his mock language. He pretended to read from the book as he muttered his nonsensical "Formosan prayers."

Psalmanazar's nonsense impressed the Bishop of London, who sent the young man to Oxford University to teach his mock language to seminarians. The seminarians were preparing to sail to Formosa as missionaries, so Psalmanazar translated the catechism into "Formosan." When distinguished linguists examined the document, they declared that Psalmanazar's nonsense was a real language; they reasoned that such a young man could not have made it up.

A Jesuit who had recently returned from traveling in Asia happened into one of Psalmanazar's lectures and challenged the impostor. Psalmanazar denounced the priest as a liar and quickly turned the audience on the priest. Psalmanazar fooled the public for a decade until someone exposed him. Impostors attract followers who have low self-esteem. Seeing an impostor exude boundless self-confidence makes his followers forget their own insecurity for a while. Hence, exposing an impostor doesn't immediately change his followers' minds. Instead, followers vent their anger on the person who reveals the truth. An impostor's fans must be left alone until they dream themselves out.

Sometimes impostors pass themselves off as members of professions that the public tends to glamorize, such as medical doctors or attorneys. When they do, they use mock professional jargon to create an illusion. Only an expert can distinguish an impostor's nonsense from actual professional terminology.

Bogus Prophecies

Nonsense has been used for bogus prophecies and fortune telling. While there are true psychics in this world, people's eagerness to read meaning into nonsense is a prime factor in the success of bogus fortunetellers. Hence, nonsense and prophecy have always gone hand in hand. For instance, unintelligible nonsense was the stock-in-trade of the ancient Greek oracle at Delphi. A prophetess sat on a bronze tripod that stood over a hole in the floor of a subterranean chamber. Ethylene gas rose through the hole, escaping from fissures deep in the earth beneath the oracle, and filled the chamber.

Oracle seekers stood outside the chamber and addressed their questions to the god Apollo. The prophetess, who was the presumed mouthpiece of Apollo, heard the questions and then inhaled ethylene. When she did, she drifted into a mildly intoxicated, trancelike state.

Ethylene is a hydrocarbon gas that was once commonly used for anesthesia. Inhaling it makes people jabber in incoherent nonsense. Hence, the prophetesses at Delphi uttered meaningless, unintelligible verbiage in response to petitioners' questions.

Resident expert interpreters were stationed outside the chamber. They listened intently, trying their best to make sense of what Apollo was saying, and then they reworked the prophetess's meaningless nonsense into semi-intelligible verses known as enigmas, or riddles. The enigmas left petitioners wondering what they meant. Hence, Delphi oracles became a watchword for obscurity. Nevertheless, the oracle was a major force in history, and it directly influenced decisions that shaped Western civilization. Evidently it *is* important to understand the role of nonsense in prophecy.

The typology of nonsense helps explain the prophecies of some renowned seers. We have identified and described multiple types of deliberate nonsense. Therefore, we can now identify those types, even when they occur in prophetic writings, which are purportedly meaningful and intelligible. This technique reveals the truth about one of the most famous fortune-tellers of history: Nostradamus.

Some claimed that Nostradamus's prophecies were nonsense, even during his lifetime. That is still a standard criticism of Nostradamus's writings, although until now, there has been no rational method to definitively prove it. The typology of nonsense provides such a method. Specifically, analysis of the selections below demonstrates that Nostradamus's writings used categorical nonsense, nonsense names, non-referential pronouns, figurative nonsense, non-junctive nonsense, and numerative nonsense, all indicated in italics.

Categorical nonsense:

> The divine word will give to the substance,
> Including heaven, earth, gold hidden in the *mystic milk*[65]

---

65   Leoni, *Nostradamus and His Prophecies*, 193.

193

Nonsense name:

> The Religion of the name of the seas will win out
> Against the sect of the son of *"Adaluncatif"*[66]

> *"Samarobryn"* one hundred leagues from the
>   hemisphere[67]

> A just one will be sent back again into exile,
> Through pestilence to the confines of *"Nonseggle"*[68]

Non-referential pronoun:

> *They* will live without law exempt from politics.[69]

> To near the Lake of Geneva will *it* be conducted,
> By the foreign maiden wishing to betray the city.[70]

Figurative nonsense and non-junctive nonsense:

> His replay to the red one will cause him to be misled,
> The King withdrawing to *the Frog and the Eagle*.[71]

Numerative nonsense:

> The blood of the just will commit a fault at London,
> Burnt through lightning of *twenty threes the six*[72]

---

66 Leoni, *Nostradamus and His Prophecies*, 441.

67 Ibid., 281.

68 Ibid., 293.

69 Ibid.

70 Ibid., 253.

71 Ibid.

72 Ibid., 177.

Of Paris bridge, Lyons wall Montpellier,
After *six hundreds and seven score three pairs*.[73]

Non-junctive nonsense:

The stubborn, lamented sect will be afraid
Of the two wounded by *A and A*.[74]

The mental effect of these verses is like that of other nonsense writings we have studied. They stimulate a flow of odd mental images, half-formed ideas, and fragmentary chains of thought. Such nonsense verses taunt the mind. Hence, Nostradamus's prophecies inspired volume upon volume of learned interpretations, yet Nostradamians seldom agree in their interpretations of particular prophecies.

One Nostradamian maintained that the nonsense name "Samorobryn" referred to Sam R. O'Brien, an American space station astronaut of the 1970s. Other commentators were intrigued with "supelman," another of Nostradamus's nonsense names. Apparently, they conjectured that it might refer to Superman, the cartoon character.

Nostradamus wrote other prophecies that are intelligible but vague. Such prophecies are abstract formulas that invite readers to use their own imagination to fill in the blanks.

These vague prophecies are so nonspecific that they are bound to come true eventually. The two prophecies below are examples:

73   Leoni, *Nostradamus and His Prophecies*, 207.
74   Ibid., 441.

Two royal brothers will wage war so fiercely
That between them the war will be so mortal
That both will occupy the strong places:
Their great quarrel will fill realm and life.[75]

Some of those most lettered in the celestial facts
Will be condemned by illiterate princes:
Punished by Edict, hunted, like criminals,
And put to death wherever they will be found.[76]

This is a highly effective method for writing tantalizing prophecies, for when a vague but meaningful prophecy comes true, it lends credibility to the nonsensical prophecies. Apparent confirmation of a vague prophecy drives Nostradamians to work harder to uncover the "true meaning" of the unintelligible prophecies.

Accordingly, this is additional evidence that nonsense interacts dynamically with meaningful language. That is, nonsense sometimes acts synergistically with meaningful language to produce enhanced, combined effects. For instance, earlier we saw that this effect occurs in nursery rhymes like "Hickory Dickory Dock." The nonsense line is placed at the beginning and end, and when the nursery rhyme is recited without its nonsensical part, it falls flat. Hence, in nursery rhymes, the nonsense energizes the meaningful part. In Nostradamus's writings, though, the meaningful prophecies energize the nonsensical ones.

---

75 Leoni, *Nostradamus and His Prophecies*, 219.

76 Ibid., 225.

Other prophets employed this same technique of mixing nonsensical and meaningful language. For example, Robert Nixon was born in England in 1467. He was an illiterate farmhand who had a habit of talking nonsense to himself as he plowed the fields. One day he suddenly stopped plowing and began giving a blow-by-blow account of a heated battle. Everyone assumed that it was a battle in his own mind that was bothering him. Later, however, the bystanders learned that a battle that matched Nixon's description had been taking place at the same time far away. So, thereafter, Nixon was regarded as a seer. Some of his recorded prophecies are displayed below. Here we see the same interweaving of vague but meaningful prophecies with others that are nonsense.

Vague but meaningful:

> A great man shall come into England,
> But the son of a King
> Shall take from him the victory.[77]

Figurative nonsense:

> *The cock of the North* shall be made to flee,
> And his feather be plucked for his pride,
> That he shall almost curse the day that he was born.[78]

---

77   Mackay, *Memoirs of Extraordinary Popular Delusions*, 199.

78   Ibid., 199–200.

Vague but meaningful:

> Through our own money and our men,
> Shall a dreadful war begin.[79]

Non-junctive nonsense:

> Between *the sickle and the suck,*
> All England shall have a pluck.[80]

Numerative nonsense:

> *Between seven, eight, and nine,*[81]

Numerative nonsense:

> In England wonders shall be seen;
> *Between nine and thirteen*
> All sorrow shall be done![82]

In an exercise, my students wrote their own nonsense prophecies after studying those of Nostradamus and Robert Nixon. Often, the students' nonsensical prognostications were indistinguishable from those of renowned seers. Completing the exercise enabled the students to reflect on how the mind processes prophetic writings.

---

79   Mackay, *Memoirs of Extraordinary Popular Delusions*, 200.

80   Ibid.

81   Ibid.

82   Ibid.

Totalitarian Control

Nonsense has been used for enforcing totalitarian rule. The idea of governments using nonsense to repress people is better known as a literary theme than as historical reality. George Orwell wrote two novels in which dictatorships employed nonsensical formulas for political control. In *1984,* an authoritarian figure known as Big Brother indoctrinated the public with meaningless slogans such as "War is Peace," "Love is Hate," and "Freedom is Slavery." The nonsensical proclamations induced a mental state known as doublethink, in which people would assent to two directly opposite and contradictory ideas at the same time. Apparently, bombarding people with nonsense numbed their minds into submission.

In Orwell's *Animal Farm*, barnyard animals took over after a farmer died and instituted a government among themselves. The liberated animals' charter for self-government began by stating, "All animals are equal." However, pigs gradually outmaneuvered other creatures and gained political control. They amended the charter to say, "All animals are equal, but some animals are more equal than others."

Marxist ideology, which dominated the Soviet Union for seventy years, was built partly on formulaic precepts that made no sense. For instance, the slogan "Property is theft!" —coined by French anarchist Pierre-Joseph Proudhon— became a popular slogan among members of the Communist Party, yet the words of the statement simply cancel each other out in a memorable self-contradiction. That is, equating property with theft destroys the meanings of both terms. Nevertheless, the meaningless slogan resonated strongly with fiery revolutionary sentiments that were prevalent at the time.

Benito Mussolini's Fascist regime in Italy used nonsensical chants at mass rallies to promote social bonding. People would recite a chant of nonsense syllables. The chant was unintelligible nonsense, but it supposedly helped bind Fascists to their leader and to the state.

Even in free democratic societies, officials may lapse into talking nonsense when they are under pressure to downplay embarrassing bungles. For example, after a seemingly senseless attack on a village in Vietnam, the United States Army needed to explain the action. A spokesman said, "It became necessary to destroy the village in order to save it."

Mock Profundity

Nonsense has been used for projecting an illusion of profundity. Some eminent intellectuals had a knack for writing nonsense that sounds profound. For example, Jacques Derrida (1930–2004) started an academic craze known as deconstruction, which was based solely on nonsense definitions and obscure, meaningless verbiage. Derrida gained legions of swooning followers who were impressed by his nonsensical pronouncements such as "Thinking is what we already know we have not yet begun."[83] He laced his lectures with enigmatic nonsense like "Oh, my friends, there is no friend."[84]

Professors at major American universities fell under Derrida's spell. Graduate students wrote profound-sounding dissertations to elucidate his incoherent musings. Pretty soon, aspiring students had to master this kind of nonsense writing to get their degrees. In other words, Derrida and his followers talked nonsense as a technique of intellectual posturing.

Purportedly, deconstruction invalidated all literary, philosophical, political, and historical works. Derrida explained that such works were devoid of truth or meaning because of inherent confusions and contradictions in language. Deconstruction got caught up in its own sweeping generalization, for Derrida's work itself is a literary, historical, and philosophical text, such as deconstruction attacks. That means that deconstruction itself is devoid of truth and meaning. In other words, deconstruction invalidated itself.

Deconstruction was based solely on nonsense definitions, and Derrida and his devotees were never able to give a coherent, meaningful definition of it. For example, he tried once again in 1993 when he lectured at a law school in New York. He said, "Needless to say, one more time, deconstruction, if there is such a thing, takes place as the experience of the impossible."[85]

---

83   Derrida, *Of Grammatology*, 93.

84   Powell, *Jacques Derrida*, 200.

85   Kandell, "Jacques Derrida, Abstruse Theorist, Dies at 74."

Pseudo-profound nonsense can also be created by cap-italizing abstract words and putting them together into grammatical sentences. Words like "being," "pure," "abso-lute," "unity," "the One," "transcendent," "immanent," and "essence" work well for writing this type of profound-sound-ing nonsense. Throwing in phrases like "in itself" helps, too. The formula results in sentences like "Being-in-itself is the pure essence of transcendent Unity." Or "The Absolute is immanent in pure being." Such sentences sound profound, but the sound of profoundness is all there is to them. Hegel and Heidegger are examples of philosophers who gained fame by mastering that kind of nonsense writing.

In my courses on nonsense, I explained this pattern to my students. Then, in an exercise, they tried writing nonsense of this type. Once they learned the rules of formulation, they were able to write sentences of pseudo-profound nonsense that were indistinguishable from those of eminent philoso-phers.

Even so, reading pseudo-profound nonsense gives some readers an agreeable experience of thinking deep thoughts. That experience may even sometimes stimulate their minds to come up with a worthwhile idea. For example, a friend of mine who is a renowned psychotherapist and scholar of world religions reported that very effect. In graduate school he read many tomes by famous authors of pseudo-profound nonsense. Even then, he said, he realized that the writings were unintelligible nonsense, yet he also acknowledged that reading those authors played an important role in his intellectual development. As C. J. Lichtenberg said, "Trying to make sense of impenetrable nonsense sometimes inspires exciting new ideas."

Pseudoscientific Theories

Pseudoscience is a form of mock professional jargon. Specifically, pseudoscience is nonsense that is modeled on scientific discourse. The works of George F. Gillette (1875–1948), one of America's great crackpots, are a prime example of pseudoscientific writings. Gillette's self-published books, including *Orthodox Oxen* and *Rational, Non-Mystical Cosmos*, are filled with nonsense definitions, categorical nonsense, and numerative nonsense.

Gillette was insanely jealous of Albert Einstein and Einstein's theory of relativity. Gillette propounded his own competing theory of the spiral universe and "back screwing theory of gravity." Gillette never defined the fundamental unit of his theory—the indivisible "unimote." Instead, he built on the notion by claiming that the universe is a "supraunimote," while the cosmos is the "maximote."

Gillette went on to add that the "ultimote" is the "Nth sub-universe plane." Gillette also said, "Gravitation is naught but that reaction in the form of sub-planar solar systems screwing through higher plane masses." Furthermore, he held that "each ultimote is simultaneously an integral part of zillions of otherplane units and only thus is its *infinite* allplane velocity and energy subdivided into zillions of *finite* planar quotas of velocity and energy."

Gillette was convinced that his nonsensical musings made perfect sense. While they may sound like scientific writings to a layperson, scientists would understand that Gillette's theory is unintelligible nonsense, although they might be unable to prove it. However, the typology developed in this book provides a rational method of demonstrating that Gillette's works contain nonsense definitions, categorical nonsense, and numerative nonsense.

Self-Deception

As Robert Frost said with self-depreciating humor, "Forgive me my nonsense as I also forgive the nonsense of those who think they talk sense." John Kenneth Galbraith said with sarcastic irony that "it is a far, far better thing to have a firm anchor in nonsense than to set out on the troubled seas of thought." Jacques Barzun said with dark foreboding that "intellect deteriorates after every surrender to folly. Unless we consciously resist, the nonsense does not pass by us, but into us." All three authors said the same thing: namely, that people sometimes use nonsense to deceive themselves. Literary critic A. S. Byatt elaborated on that theme in her novel *Babel Tower*. A male character reflecting on his male relatives' religious obsessions concluded that

> It is possible for human beings to spend the whole of
> their lives on nonsense. And not only that, but perhaps
> there was a trap, a quirk, a temptation in the nature
> of language itself that led people, that induced them to
> spend the whole of their lives on nonsense.

Others might maintain that the notion of self-deception is self-contradictory. After all, the idea of deceiving somebody seems to involve keeping something secret from that person. How, though, could one keep a secret from oneself? The concept does not seem to make sense.

Even so, as a psychiatrist and people-watcher, I concede that people do sometimes seem to deceive themselves. That is, people have mental mechanisms whereby they keep themselves in the dark about things that they are clearly in a position to know.

Perhaps self-deception also plays a role in other misuses of nonsense: imposture, fortunetelling, totalitarian control, intellectual posturing, and pseudoscience. Evidently, nonsense sometimes hijacks mental machinery that is ordinarily responsible for logical thinking and intelligent judgment. In that regard, the theory of nonsense can be a useful adjunct for guiding critical thinking.

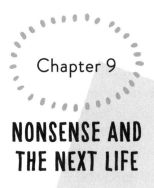

Chapter 9

NONSENSE AND THE NEXT LIFE

Whereas it is permissible, in our language, to speak of a man as surviving a complete loss of memory or a complete change of character, it is self-contradictory to speak of a man as surviving the annihilation of his body.

A. J. Ayer,
Language, Truth and Logic

We have gone on a pilgrimage through the fascinating parallel world of nonsense. Now we are ready to circle back to the biggest question of human existence: the prospect of life after death. This chapter applies some specific principles we have learned to formulate a new understanding of what happens when we die. We will see how our new knowledge about nonsense definitions, nonsensical magic words, and nonsense travel narratives clarifies the notion of an afterlife. We will learn how the logic of nonsense gives rise to a simple, reliable technique for communing with the spirits of our departed loved ones, and we will comprehend a bold new rational method for investigating near-death experiences.

Nonsense of several distinct types constitutes the notion of life after death. Early in the twentieth century, some analytic philosophers raised what then seemed a telling, even decisive objection to philosophical inquiry into life after death. Their objection reputedly precluded further rational investigation of perhaps the biggest question of human existence and a problem with a long history in philosophy. Pythagoras, Heraclitus, Parmenides, Empedocles, Plato, Democritus, and Epicurus, for example, addressed the question in their philosophies, yet that philosophical tradition seemingly came to an end when analytic philosophers contended that the notion of life after death is unverifiable, unintelligible nonsense.

That was analytic philosophy's standard objection to ancient philosophical problems, of course. Various eminent analytic philosophers discussed the view that discussion about an afterlife is meaningless and unintelligible. The English philosopher C. D. Broad, for example, said that some philosophers "concluded that it is simply meaningless to talk of a human personality surviving the death of its body."[86]

---

86   Broad, *Lectures on Psychical Research*, 302.

Similarly, the Welsh philosopher H. H. Price said:

> If we are to discuss the problem of survival intelligently, we must try to form some idea of what the life after death might conceivably be like. If we cannot form such an idea, however rough and provisional, it is pointless to discuss the factual evidence for or against the "Survival Hypothesis." A critic may object that there is no such hypothesis, on the grounds that the phrase "survival of human personality after death" has no intelligible meaning at all.[87]

Philosopher C. J. Ducasse also posed the question whether or not the notion of life after death is intelligible, pointing out that

> Persons who are convinced that "the human personality survives bodily death," or convinced that it does not, or who are curious as to whether or not it does, are in fact in the position of being full of curiosity or conviction as to they know not just what! Evidently, so long as one does not know just what one means by the phrase "the personality's survival after death," one cannot tell what kinds of observable facts would or would not constitute evidence of such survival. Persons who use the phrase usually think they know well enough what they mean by it. But this is only because they have never adequately considered the diversity of meanings confounded under that wishful vague phrase.

---

87 Price, *Philosophical Interactions with Parapsychology*, 263.

Analytic philosophers were following in the footsteps of David Hume (1711–1776), a Scottish historian and relentlessly skeptical empiricist philosopher. Hume's insights into causality and inductive reasoning helped shape the scientific mind. Hume identified and eloquently stated the primary problem that stands in the way of genuine rational inquiry into the prospect of an afterlife. Specifically, he acknowledged that the question of life after death does not mesh with the principles of ordinary Aristotelian logic:

> By the mere light of reason it seems difficult to prove the Immortality of the Soul...By what arguments or analogies can we prove any state of existence, which no one ever saw, and which no way resembles any that ever was seen?...Some new species of logic is requisite for that purpose, and some new faculties of the mind that they may enable us to comprehend that logic.[88]

Hume's famous criterion probably was an ironic statement. That is, he probably meant that rational proof of life after death is impossible. After all, ordinary Aristotelian logic has served us well for more than two thousand years, and we usually assume that we know our minds well. How likely does it seem that there could be unknown faculties of the mind?

The rational principles of nonsense that this book developed can be roughly characterized as a new kind of logic, however. Furthermore, the sense of nonsense can be plau-

---

88   Hume, *Essays and Treatises on Various Subjects*, 226, 229.

sibly characterized as a previously unknown faculty of the mind. We are in a somewhat better position than were Ayer, Broad, Price, Ducasse, et.al., to judge whether the notion of an afterlife is unintelligible.

Calling an idea unintelligible, and thereby dismissing it, is part of the landscape of scientific, academic, and religious debate. Previously, however, there was no clear rational method for resolving disagreements over whether or not an idea is unintelligible. Now, however, our typology of nonsense engenders a method for settling some such disagreements, for if a disputed idea matches a previously established type of nonsense, that proves that the idea is unintelligible nonsense. This chapter applies that method to prove positively that the notion of life after death is a complex form of nonsense in the following specific ways.

Nonsense definitions underlie stock phrases that collectively express the notion of the life after death. The sentence "There is life after death" is an outright self-contradiction,- for "death" means the final, irreversible cessation of life. Yet when I spring this fact on people in face-to-face conversations, it takes them by surprise. They get flustered, but they are forced to admit that it is true.

Still, as we saw earlier, people try to correct themselves when they realize that they have been talking nonsense unknowingly. They attempt to put what they had been trying to say into some other words that *do* make sense. So, when they realize that talking about life after death is self-contra-dictory, they substitute some other supposedly synonymous expression.

In this case, however, the technique does not work, for all the other common language expressions that are supposedly interchangeable with "life after death" are nonsense, too, by our own established definitions and criteria.

For example, some prefer "survival of bodily death." Why does the word "bodily" appear in this phrase? "Death" already includes the notion of there being a body that dies, so the "bodily" is superfluous, except perhaps to soften the self-contradiction. "Survival of death" shocks the mind and is brazenly self-contradictory. This shocking self-contradic-tion is the power behind Woody Allen's famous joke, "If you can survive death, you can survive just about anything."

To survive something is to get through it without dying, so it makes no sense to talk of someone surviving death, whether the qualifier "bodily" is added or not. We are not provided with an explanation about what any supposed dif-ferences between regular death and "bodily" death might be.

We can substitute familiar expressions of supposedly equivalent meaning; we can use the word "beyond," for example, and say, "There is life beyond death." So, here, instead of a bold self-contradiction, we have a mystifying spatial metaphor. That is, there is no literal sense in which life could be "beyond" death, yet no clear metaphoric mean-ing is established, either.

Moreover, "after" expresses a temporal relationship and "beyond" expresses a spatial relationship. Upon reflection, then, it seems strange that the phrases "life after death" and "life beyond death" are used as synonyms. So, instead, we move on by substituting purely spatial phrases like "the world beyond" or "the beyond" or "the other side."

These are spatial terms but not spatial concepts. "The world beyond" does not exist in any defined spatial relationship to the present world. Thus, we cannot point to the beyond, for example, if someone asks us to do it. The request simply makes no sense.

"The other side" is equally problematic, for there is no clear answer available for the next logical question, namely, "The other side of what?" "The other side" suggests a dividing line or barrier separating two spaces, yet nothing whatsoever indicates in which direction "the other side" supposedly lies from this world.

So, "the world beyond death," "the beyond," "the other side," and the like are not literal in meaning, but they are not meaningful, intelligible metaphors, either. Although they resemble metaphors, there is no way of telling what their supposed literal meanings might be. In other words, we cannot specify equivalent literal meanings for supposed spatial metaphors like "the world beyond death." Consequently, by the criteria established earlier, phrases such as "the beyond" and "the other side" are nonsense metaphors.

The idea of an afterlife is not yet a full-fledged concept. Rather, it is a loose conglomeration of self-contradictions and figurative nonsense such as meaningless, unintelligible spatial metaphors. Plenty of other nonsensical metaphors and other nonsensical figures of speech are also used for verbalizing the idea of an afterlife. For example, death is sometimes likened to an expansion of consciousness or an ascension to a higher plane of consciousness. Here again, however, we are falling back on spatial metaphors that have no equivalent literal meanings that can be specified.

Whatever figure of speech anyone uses for the afterlife, however, the essential problem remains the same. Namely, the figures of speech are never linked to equivalent literal meanings. Therefore, the nebulous notion of life after death is a complex mixture of self-contradictions and figurative nonsense. Nevertheless, as we know, nonsense stimulates a flow of odd mental imagery, half-formed ideas, and fragmentary chains of thought, so phrases like "life after death" and "the world beyond" evoke plenty of jumbled mental images, garbled half-thoughts, and incoherent or distorted mentation—and we mistake that for a concept of the afterlife. Moreover, adding to the confusion, we shift indifferently and casually from one of these words or phrases to another until we make a complete circle. Our minds get lost amidst enthralling but foggy images and half-formed notions, and we take for granted that these familiar words and phrases have a determinable literal meaning.

We glide smoothly from "life after death" to "the world beyond death" to "the next life" to "the afterlife" and so on. We readily interchange self-contradictory phrases with assorted figurative nonsense. The ease of substituting one supposedly equivalent phrase for another heightens the illusion that these literally meaningless, unintelligible expressions somehow make sense.

The circular process of substituting nonsense for nonsense does not amount to a meaningful, intelligible definition of "life after death." Instead, we recognize it as a new sub-type of nonsense definition. That conclusion follows from the long process of discovery and reasoning in which we have been engaged, so the core notion of life after death is nonsense after all, just as various eminent thinkers have said.

Therefore, sentences like "Is there a life after death?" are nonsense questions. We already saw that nonsense questions play a crucial role in religion as well as in scientific inquiry. Asking whether or not there is an afterlife is part and parcel of being a human being. In religion and the spiritual life, the idea of a life after death is an enduring source of hope and inspiration. Like other important nonsense questions, the question of life after death also constantly stimulates rational inquiry and debate.

Nonsense concerning life after death may sometimes arise from the mind's attempts to escape the reality of death. Earlier, we learned that people sometimes talk nonsense because of severe stress. They may talk incoherent nonsense when their minds are racing as they are trying to escape situations of mortal danger. Hence, soldiers sometimes talk incoherent nonsense upon being rescued from horrific battles in which they narrowly escaped death or life-threatening injury. In such cases, nonsense is the mind's last-ditch attempt to escape imminent death.

Speculating about life after death may sometimes also be partly an attempt to evade the reality of death. In other words, in trying to escape death, the mind may contradict itself, pose nonsense questions, and create nonsensical figures of speech.

Speculative books about life after death have been enormously popular since antiquity. Reading such books is a pleasurable way of escaping one's anxieties about death. Similarly, Houdini entertained audiences with death-defying escapes from seemingly inescapable predicaments. He seriously pondered the question of life after death and even promised to try communicating from the other side, if there were an afterlife. Hence, popular books about life after death and Houdini's entertaining escapades attest to the same principle: namely, life after death would be an ultimate form of escape—an escape from the space-time continuum itself.

Nonsense occurred in magical formulas that once supposedly transported people temporarily to a world beyond death. Earlier, we discussed the ancient belief that uttering the right combination of exotic nonsense could magically alter reality. Similarly, it was also believed that formulaic nonsense words could open a doorway between this world and an afterlife world. In other words, nonsense once symbolized the transition from physical reality into a transcendent afterlife reality.

Shamans supposedly transported themselves across the Great Divide by singing songs that mixed nonsense with meaningful language to produce a unified effect. Shamanic songs consisted of nonsense syllables and meaningless refrains combined with meaningful, intelligible parts. Certain shamans of Siberia would shout, "By the power of our songs, we cross it!" in the middle of their performances. That would signify to the audience that the shaman had at that point crossed the barrier into the spirit world.

Nonsense was not just a one-way street, however, that went only to the other side. For the magical, cross-dimensional effect of nonsense also worked in the opposite direction. The right nonsense could sometimes pull the departed from the spirit world back to this world.

Nonsense occurred in magical formulas that once supposedly called spirits back from a world beyond. The Greek Magical Papyri contained instructions for contacting the dead in the afterlife world. The procedure required someone who wanted to call up the spirit of a deceased person to utter specific, strange-sounding nonsense words. Uttering the mysterious magical nonsense formula of "SOUTHOU BERBROI AKTEROBORE GERIE" would supposedly call up an apparition of a departed individual.

Nonsense was also used at ancient Greek oracles to make spirits of the dead visible and audible to spectators. Lucian of Samosota poked fun at oracles of the dead and the exotic, meaningless nonsense that was used there to summon spirits. Lucian said that evokers of spirits uttered strange polysyllabic, foreign-sounding words that made no sense.

Using nonsense to summon the dead is also sometimes a theme of popular entertainment. For example, the movie *Beetlejuice* is a dark comedy about a haunting. In the movie, a medium called up spirits of the dead by uttering the following nonsensical combination of words:

> Hands vermillion
> Start of five
> Bright cotillion
> Ravens dive
> Nightshade's promise
> Spirits strive
> To the living
> Let now the dead come alive.[89]

Incredible as it may seem, nonsense can actually be used successfully to induce visionary reunions with the deceased. I know because I re-created the ancient process. I guided hundreds of people through a procedure during which they experienced vivid, lifelike apparitions of their departed loved ones. The procedure I devised has been replicated by mul-

---

89 Michael McDowell, Warren Skaaren, and Larry Wilson, *Beetlejuice* (1988).

tiple independent investigators with the same remarkable results.[90]

I reconstructed this procedure by combing two sources. I read ancient historical and magic texts that describe how to evoke spirits of the deceased. I also studied archeological reports of excavating the most famous of the ancient Greek oracles of the dead. Putting those two sources of information together made it plain how the process worked.

Ancient historical and literary texts reveal that formulaic nonsense was a key component of procedures for preparing people's minds for experiencing apparitions. Meanwhile, archeological findings showed that apparitions appeared in reflective surfaces such as mirrors, polished metal bowls, or pools of clear water. That detail uncovers a psychological principle involved in the operation of the oracle of the dead.

Gazing into the optical depth of a mirror, crystal ball, or pool of clear water often induces fantastical iridescent visions. Gazers report seeing majestic landscapes, mountains, forests, lakes, and rivers. They also report seeing faces of people moving around in complex settings such as inside buildings or on a street. The images appear lifelike, with essentially photographic reality. The images often have bright, beautiful, lively colors, and they appear and take on a life of their own irrespective of the gazer's conscious volition.

---

90 For example, see Edward Hastings, Michael Hutton, William Braud, et. al., "Psychomanteum Research: Experiences and Effects on Bereavement," *Omega Journal of Death and Dying* (1 November 2002), https://doi.org/10.2190/LV5G-E3JV-6CVT-FKN5.

The images usually appear to be three-dimensional, and they move around on their own accord.

I constructed a simple apparitions chamber where people could experience realistic interactive visions of deceased loved ones. You can try this for yourself by following simple instructions.

EXERCISE

Induce Visionary Reunions with the Deceased

Choose a small room, such as a well-ventilated walk-in closet. Paint the walls of the room flat black or cover the walls and ceiling of the room with a black fabric known as teeshot poplin.

Obtain a wall mirror the sides of which are about three or four feet in height and width. Place a comfortable chair on the floor about three feet in front of the mirror on the wall. Choose a chair with a back that reclines slightly backwards so that you can relax comfortably.

Position the mirror high enough on the wall so that you cannot see your reflection when looking upward from the chair. Obtain a small plug-in lamp with a little light bulb, say about the size of a ping pong ball or smaller and place the lamp behind the chair. You might add a rheostat (a dimmer switch) in the circuit and place the switch where you can easily reach it from the chair. That way, you can adjust the light in the darkened chamber to your own comfort level. This requires trial and error to achieve your optimal level.

That is all the physical apparatus you need to commune with your deceased relatives and friends. Completing a

*psychological and spiritual procedure is needed to prepare
your mind for perceiving and interacting with spirits in your
apparition chamber. Nonsense was an integral element of
ancient techniques for calling up the spirits of the deceased.
Choose some work of nonsense that speaks to you and strongly
affects your consciousness. You might choose a favorite nonsense
poem, for instance, or a particularly mind-bending book by Dr.
Seuss. Keep the work of nonsense close at hand so that you can
read it shortly before entering the apparition chamber.*

*Choose some deceased person known to you that you would
like to see again. Call up your poignant memories of this
person. Ask yourself what your most pleasant memories of this
individual are and also reflect on the unpleasant memories,
the conflicts, and any unfinished business. Looking at old
photographs of the person might help. Take your time and go
through the process thoughtfully, feeling the emotions.*

*If you are a loner and homebody like me, you might prefer
to try this procedure by yourself. Otherwise, choose a friend to
help you through the process. Your friend can ask you questions
about the deceased person you want to see. That will stir up
your memories and feelings about your relationship with your
deceased loved one. Don't hurry and don't skip any steps.*

*Continue the process of reflection until you have brought
your memories and feelings about your deceased loved one
vividly before your mind. Then read aloud the work of nonsense
that you selected. That will help shift your consciousness to a
state in which you can more readily perceive and experience
apparitions of the deceased.*

*Once you have completed all those steps, enter your
darkened apparition chamber and sit down. Switch on the
light and adjust the illumination with the dimmer switch. Get
comfortable in the chair and relax deeply. Gaze into the depths
of the mirror and let the memories and feelings you experienced
during the preparation process flow through your mind.*

Plan to spend at least an hour in the chamber during your first attempt. People who experience apparitions often say that they first see clouds, fog, or mists form in the mirror. More defined images or visions then appear. Some people say that a three-dimensional vision of their departed relative or friend forms in the mirror. Others say that the apparition then steps out of the mirror and emerges into the room. Yet others say that their consciousness goes through the mirror into a parallel reality where they meet departed loved ones.

About 30 percent of subjects report hearing the audible voice of the deceased during their experience. Almost all the rest report experiencing heart-to-heart or mind-to-mind communication or conversations with their loved ones. Most report a vivid sense of presence of their loved ones during the encounter.

. . . .

My book *Reunions* (Villard Publishers, 1993) covers my research in greater detail. Classical scholar Daniel Ogden's book *Greek and Roman Necromancy* (Princeton University Press, 2001) is a fascinating history of oracles of the dead. Ogden's book discusses how evocation of the deceased influenced the origins of Western thought in ancient Greek philosophy.

Nonsense as a Comedic Gateway

Nonsense has been used in jokes, cartoons, and songs to denote the entrance into a world beyond death. The idea of nonsense at the gateway between this life and the next life is also a familiar theme of popular entertainment. Singer Shirley Ellis's "The Clapping Song" was a hit in the 1950s. The song combined a nonsense chant with hand clapping. People in the audience would clap their hands in a certain sequence in time with the singer's words and music. Again, here is an example of nonsense chanted by a group, along with physical activity, to forge or strengthen social bonds.

In the late 1960s, a cartoon in the *Saturday Review of Literature* featured a colossal nonsensical diagram of the entranceway to heaven. In the cartoon, two men had just arrived in heaven and, newly transformed into angels, they stood side by side, surveying the scene. They gazed upward toward a vast, complex geometrical diagram in the distance that dominated the landscape. The diagram looked like those that are found in the later chapters of high school geometry textbooks.

Each line, tangent, circle, or triangle in the diagram was labeled with a different abstract term. Hence, the diagram contained a meaningless, unintelligible mish-mash of words such as "truth," "charity," "love," "justice," "wisdom," "holiness," and so on. To designate the enormous geometrical diagram, there appeared beneath it the words THE MEANING OF LIFE.

Heidegger and a Hippopotamus Arrived at the Pearly Gates is a book that uses jokes to explain philosophical ideas about the afterlife. The title refers to one of the book's jokes. Heidegger—whose philosophical writings were notoriously obscure, if not unintelligible—and a hippopotamus faced St. Peter at the same time. St. Peter would allow only one of them past the Pearly Gates, so he asked each of them for some sort of reason to let them in. Heidegger spoke first and said:

223

> To think Being itself explicitly requires disregarding
> Being to the extent that it is only grounded and inter-
> preted in terms of beings and for beings as their ground,
> as in all metaphysics.

St. Peter immediately turned Heidegger away and admit-
ted the hippopotamus into heaven by default. The joke
reversed the normal situation, for talking nonsense typically
gets someone across to the other side. In the joke, though,
Heidegger was excluded from heaven because he talked nonsense. In sum, ancient magical beliefs about nonsense are
somehow preserved in popular culture through cartoons,
humor, and songs.

Nonsensical Questions about Death and Justice

Nonsense modeled on worldly justice systems is central to
many people's notions of life after death. Bereaved people
often ask where their deceased loved ones are. They ask this
plaintively, sincerely, from the bottoms of their hearts. They
ask this, knowing full well where the body was buried or
where the ashes were scattered. Asking "Where?" is a normal part of the grieving process.

Yet, in reality, it does not make intelligible sense to ask
where a deceased person is. Asking where my dead grandfather is, for example, is simply meaningless and unintelligible.
Still, questions like that automatically arise from within us
during periods of grief. Apparently, the subconscious mind

does not distinguish clearly between death and departure or abandonment. "Where is my deceased grandfather?" is a nonsense question. Yet, like meaningful "Where?" questions, it presupposes a spatial frame of reference. That is, it calls for an answer in spatial terms.

Furthermore, although asking where a dead person is is meaningless and unintelligible, it still may convey considerable imperative force. We may feel pressure to come up with an answer, even knowing that it is a nonsense question. The mind feels compelled to provide some sort of place description to satisfy persistent, nagging questions about where dead people are.

Earlier, we saw that formatting unintelligible language as a place description can create a convincing inner sense of another world. Such nonsense worlds cannot be, except in words. Yet, some nonsense worlds exert a strong hold on the human mind.

Heaven and hell are many religious people's answers to "Where?" questions concerning the dead. In effect, heaven and hell are places where the dead still live. But in what direction do these places lie, and how far distant are they? These questions are unmanageable because they make no intelligible sense. The universe contains the only space we know anything about, and heaven and hell do not exist in an intelligible spatial relationship to the universe.

Furthermore, heaven and hell are nonsense worlds modeled on worldly systems of justice—reward and punishment.

However, eternal reward and punishment are dispensed in heaven and hell, which is a nonsensical system of justice. Their sheer unintelligible everlastingness removes heaven and hell from the category of justice and puts them in the category of nonsense.

The idea of justice includes a proportionality between an act and its consequent reward or punishment. A human life spans a few decades, which is insignificant compared to the supposed infinite billions of trillions of eons of eternity. Whatever someone did during that brief span of time, though, is supposedly subject to an everlasting, eternal, unending reward or punishment in heaven or hell. Therefore, notions of supposed eternal heavenly or hellish rewards or punishments bear no intelligible relationship to the concept of justice. In other words, heaven and hell are a form of nonsense built around the idea of a justice system.

Ancient Greek Nonsense and EVP

Nonsense is inherent in the notion of life after death. This chapter has presented evidence that the notion is a complex conjoining and comingling of multiple distinct types of nonsense. The association between nonsense and the afterlife traces back to the origins of western thought in ancient Greece.

Homer's *Odyssey* portrays the dead leading a pale and joyless existence in the underworld. Spirits of the dead flit about and gibber since they no longer have their wits about them. Consequently, what they say makes no sense, and they ramble on in aimless, fragmented, disjointed talk. The early Greek idea that spirits of the dead talk nonsense has persisted in the background of Western thought ever since, and it occasionally resurfaces.

One branch of modern afterlife research in particular definitely embraces the traditional Greek idea. Dr. Konstantin Raudive, a psychiatrist, pioneered studies of what are known as electronic voice phenomena, or EVP. Dr. Raudive recorded the static that is heard when a radio is tuned to frequencies between the broadcast channels. He and his coworkers listened carefully to the recorded sounds, sometimes replaying the same segment of recorded static again and again. They heard what they took to be voices amidst the static and tried to transcribe them exactly. Eventually they inferred that the sounds were voices of deceased people who were trying to communicate from the other side.

Prominent EVP researchers acknowledge that messages they have heard and transcribed seem to be nonsensical. To their credit, they refrain from ascribing symbolic or mystical meanings to the enigmatic words. Instead, they accept that the messages coming from spirits on the other side are nonsensical.

The usual objections to EVP research are that voices heard in static are auditory illusions and EVP researchers indulge in wishful thinking. Indeed, it is easy to hear hisses, rustlings, and static as voices, and the more closely you listen, the more they sound like voices. Auditory illusions like that are analogous to visual illusions, known as pareidolia. When you see, say, a face in the clouds, you can point the face out to others and they will see it, too. The longer you look at such an illusion, the more real it seems, until the cloud changes shape or moves out of sight.

I will set that point aside as undisputed. Instead, I will focus on important interactions between nonsense and the mind that occur when someone thinks about life after death. I will also stipulate that I am ignorant about the subjects of radio transmission and static. I will confine my analysis to EVP researchers' comments about the nonsense they have heard.

Dr. Raudive published a book on his research, titled *Breakthrough* (Colin Smythe Publishers, 1971). The book contains page after page of meticulous transcripts of spirit voices. Many of the messages are nonsense. For instance, one of the recorded voices said, "Statowitz one man eight nought one inch rub off." Dr. Raudive and other EVP investigators realized combinations like that are nonsense, and they said so. They were more impressed by the fact that voices could be heard in static than by the fact that the voices talk nonsense. To a degree, that is as it should be.

Earlier, we discussed cross-dimensional nonsense generated when the mind switches from one framework of existence to some other framework. We might expect that messages sent from the next life would be received as unintelligible nonsense. Today's EVP researchers are still exceptionally tolerant of nonsense.

I heard a psychologist who studies EVP deliver a public lecture on the subject in 2018. He explicitly pointed out that nonsense is heard in the recorded voices. EVP research forces intellectually honest investigators to acknowledge that nonsense factors into the rational study of life after death. Accordingly, the typology we developed in earlier chapters can assist EVP researchers.

For instance, many of Dr. Raudive's original recorded communications were examples of soraismic nonsense. Soraismic nonsense, you may remember, occurs when words from more than one language are put together in an unintelligible combination. I cited the sentence "Moi, deux some fried belle in garcon, and eoufs those my glass, s'il vous plait," as an example of soraismic nonsense.

Nonsense is always close to the surface when someone thinks about life after death. When it does emerge, it should be acknowledged and analyzed rather than simply avoided or denied. EVP research is a case in point that illustrates the general principle. Nonsense inevitably enters into the equation whenever the mind thinks of life after death.

Nonsense concerning life after death functions as a placeholder in pursuing truth. The analysis in this chapter revealed nonsense at the core of the idea that there is a life beyond death. Even so, people have kept speculation about the subject afloat for thousands upon thousands of years.

The unintelligibility of the idea does not deter people from wondering about an afterlife, and the nonsense they talk about holds a place open in language and the mind.

"Is there life after death?" is a nonsense question, but people will not stop asking it. Some even try applying rational methods to answer the questions, so it is sometimes posed as a topic for academic or scientific debate or discussion. Hence, in the search for knowledge, the nonsense question of life after death is a placeholder.

Some other big questions functioned as placeholder nonsense for a long time. Talk about human flight or lunar voyages symbolized nonsense for many centuries, but both emerged as true realities through a protracted process of rational study. Still, we do not know whether the unintelligible question of an afterlife will ever emerge from a rational process as new truth and knowledge. Nor do we have any idea of how far along in the process of transmutation of nonsense into knowledge the question might be.

Suppose for the moment, however, that the afterlife does happen to be a nonsense question that someday will be transformed into new knowledge. In that case, our analysis tells us something interesting about our current status in relation to a life beyond death. Namely, our minds are now separated from the after-death world by a veil consisting of several types of unintelligible nonsense. Before, the notion of life after death was blurry, foggy, and obscure by comparison. Now, however, the fog has resolved into several separate structures, each of which we recognize from previous examples.

Specifically, the notion of an afterlife consists of self-contradictions, nonsense definitions, nonsense questions, magical nonsense, figurative nonsense, nonsense worlds, and a nonsensical justice system. Furthermore, we already studied each of those types of nonsense in constructing our typology. Hence, an analysis in terms of rational principles of nonsense provides a more detailed map of the notion of an afterlife than ordinary logic does.

Nonsense and Near-Death Experiences

Nonsense forms a mental and spiritual interface with a world beyond death. That is, enigmatic nonsense is interposed between known reality and a hypothetical unknown state of reality transcending death. Nonsense is an intermediate transitional quantity between the two realms, so it would make sense that a person who returned from a trip to the afterlife would talk nonsense about the experience.

Nonsense travel narratives are the standard format for recounting near-death experiences. Near-death experiences, which captured the attention of the public in 1976, have had significant worldwide impact since then. Many people have said that hearing or reading about near-death experiences inspired or consoled them or cured their fear of death. These experiences have made a permanent mark on popular culture through a steady stream of Hollywood movies and best-selling books. Near-death experiences are now an accepted subject of articles in respected professional journals of medicine. Some physicians have even suggested that studies of near-death experiences might provide scientific evidence of life after death.

Principles of nonsense are necessary for rational comprehension of near-death experiences. The following analysis will apply our typology of nonsense to illuminate the structure of near-death experiences. Then, we will see how knowledge about nonsense engenders a unique new method of rational inquiry into near-death experiences and life after death.

Many people who almost died from severe illnesses or injuries subsequently reported episodes of transcendent consciousness. Most of them said that their transcendent near-death experiences were ineffable, or indescribable—they could not describe their experience in words. In fact, ineffability is one of the most frequently mentioned elements in people's accounts of their spiritual experiences of almost dying.

A speaker who says that a personal transcendent experience of near death is ineffable thereby makes a stipulation that no words are adequate or that their experiences are beyond words. Hence, we must take ineffability seriously, for a claim of ineffability stipulates that the rest of the words in that account should not be taken in their ordinary senses.

In discussing the difficulty of putting near-death experiences into words, people also often stated that their experiences were not in space or time. They maintained that their transcendent consciousness took place in a timeless state, or that they did not experience the passage of time. One woman's words can stand for those of hundreds of other people who expressed the same thought. She said, "Raymond, you could say that my experience took one second and you could say that it took ten thousand years, and it wouldn't make one bit of difference which way you said it."

People who had near-death experiences often reviewed their entire life in a kind of holographic panorama that revealed their every action in detail. They reviewed everything they had ever done and experienced every one of their actions from within the consciousness of the other people with whom they interacted, yet they said that no time had passed during their life review: they saw everything in an instant. To talk about the life review at all, they were forced to recount it in a sequence since language is necessarily sequential. However, they said that they did not experience the panoramic review as a sequence. In sum, the near-death experiences purportedly take place in a timeless state of existence.

People with near-death experiences also often stated that their experiences did not take place in ordinary space. They said that the transcendent part of their near-death experiences occurred in a non-spatial frame of reference. Their near-death experiences purportedly happened in a quasi-spatial state of reality that they could not describe.

Near-death experiences, which are ineffable, take place in a timeless, non-spatial state of reality. That is a major difficulty people faced when they tried to put into words their spiritual experiences of almost dying. It seems that practically everyone figures out the same compromising solution.

Specifically, people who had near-death experiences said that they got out of their bodies and viewed the scene from above. They said they went through a dark tunnel into a bright, loving, joyful light. They said that they were reunited with their deceased loved ones in the light. They said that every action of their lives passed before them in a vivid panoramic review, and then they returned to their bodies and came back to life.

Accordingly, people recounted their indescribably ineffable, transcendent experiences of nearly dying in narrative format. Since they could not describe their experiences, they narrated the experiences instead. That does not involve a logical inconsistency since ineffability is not the same thing as inexorability. Apparently, what they could not describe, they narrated instead, or told in the form of a story.

Specifically, narratives of near-death experiences are travel narratives, or travel stories. People said they got out of their bodies, went through a tunnel into a joyful, loving world of light, and then returned to life. That format is plainly a travel narrative. However, the narrative stipulated and presupposed that the near-death experience did not take place in the time-space continuum. Furthermore, the travel narrative also stipulated that no words are adequate for describing near-death experiences.

How can travel narratives be meaningful and intelligible in relation to transcendent experiences that purportedly did not take place in time or space? Saying that an experience was not in space or time removes the necessary preconditions for a meaningful, intelligible travel narrative. Hence, familiar accounts of near-death experiences meet our previously stated criteria for nonsense travel narratives.

Hearing someone describe a near-death experience can create a vivid inner sense of motion into a world beyond death. We inwardly experience moving into a light even though we acknowledge that motion could not exist except in words. That sense of inner motion is a known effect of nonsense travel narratives.

Earlier, we learned that people who realized that they had talked nonsense inadvertently took corrective action. They tried to reword, reformulate, or modify what they said to make it intelligible. For, as a general rule, people try to make intelligible sense when they talk and avoid talking nonsense. Accordingly, possessing knowledge about nonsense, including its relationship to the notion of an afterlife, might well influence how someone recounts a subsequent near-death experience.

In other words, the rational comprehension of nonsense as a structural domain of language, mind, and spirit should affect how people recount future near-death experiences. Knowing rational principles of nonsense in advance should steer someone to recount a personal near-death experience differently, for they would understand in detail why the standard travel narrative format is unintelligible. Hence, they could be expected to shift to some other format in an attempt to make what they say intelligible.

I predict that someone's pre-existing knowledge about nonsense can interact with transcendent aspects of that person's near-death experience. The interaction should influence how that person puts a subsequent near-death experience into words. Eventually, someone who has already mastered rational principles of nonsense will happen to have a near-death experience. I predict that such people will recount their transcendent experiences of near death in some new and illuminating way.

My prediction has now been confirmed in at least one instance. In October 2015 I received a telephone call from a friend who is a distinguished artist and scientist. He had attended one of my seminars on nonsense a few years earlier. The purpose of his call was to tell me about the near-death experiences he had during a recent hospitalization.

A couple of months before his call, my friend contracted severe influenza. Gangrene developed in his leg, which had to be amputated. He was resuscitated from three cardiac arrests during his lengthy stay in the hospital. Interestingly, he did not recount his near-death experiences in the familiar travel narrative format. Instead, he described them as conversations with God. In one experience, God showed him a holographic video of his life. His conversation with God focused on a horrible family tragedy that had taken place many years earlier and affected him deeply.

My friend was still debilitated from his illness, and his voice was weak as he recounted his experiences. Suddenly, though, his voice became clear and energetic. While he was in the near-death state, he said, his mind went back to the nonsense seminar he attended. From that viewpoint, he realized that what I had said was true. As he put it, you cannot understand how that world is related to this world unless you take the unintelligibility axis into account.

Of course, we cannot draw a general conclusion from a single case. Nevertheless, the totality of considerations presented in this book convinces me that I am on the right track. Therefore, I hereby claim that my method works. The logic of nonsense reformats the mind to comprehend and articulate near-death experiences in a new, more intelligible way. I contend that my friend is the first of many that are to follow. We have a fresh, reliable, rational method for exploring the afterlife dimension through near-death experiences.

Accounts of near-death experiences given by people who previously learned the logic of nonsense may differ significantly from the familiar nonsense travel narrative format.

That format represents near-death experiences as seen through the lens of ordinary Aristotelian logic only. Someday we may have accounts of near-death experiences told through the lenses of Aristotelian logic and a supplementary logic of nonsense. Comparing these two kinds of accounts may well yield significant new insights into near-death experiences and the question of a life beyond death.

Nonsense and the Soul

Nonsense pervades notions of the soul or self that supposedly persists in the afterlife. Some would object that it is irrelevant to point to the alleged unintelligibility of ideas about an afterlife. After all, they would say, life after death has to do with the soul, and surely we know what the soul is—or do we?

In reality, saying that it is the soul or self that survives physical death does nothing to save the situation, for the soul or self is a supposedly immaterial and conscious entity that somehow serves as the subject of an individual's personal experiences. And, from long familiarity, we presuppose that the notion makes perfect sense. However, examining their history shows that notions about the soul or self are another form of placeholder nonsense. Hence, trying to rescue ideas about life after death by invoking the soul merely transfers the unintelligibility onto another word.

The question of life after death devolves into the philosophical problem of personal identity. That is, what constitutes the identity of a human individual? Plato maintained that it resides in the individual's immaterial soul, which pertains to a changeless, intelligible reality that transcends the physical world. He claimed that the body belongs to an ever-changing, unintelligible material realm that is less real by comparison and noted that "The body fills us with loves and desires and fears and all sorts of fancies and a great deal of nonsense."[91]

Modern thought upended Plato's ideas and identified the physical world with intelligibility and the soul with unintelligible nonsense. For instance, David Hume described the difficulty of getting a handle on the slippery notion of a core self. Hume said,

> When I enter most intimately into what I call myself, I always stumble on some particular perception or other, of heat or cold, light or shade, love or hatred, pain or pleasure. (I never can catch myself at any time without a perception, and never can observe any thing but the perception....)[92]

Today's neuroscientists have no better luck pinpointing the elusive notion of a core self. In other words, the idea seems obvious at first, but it dissolves into unintelligible nonsense when we try to put it into a clear formulation. The problem of a life after death cannot be solved without a corresponding solution to the problem of personal identity.

91 Plato, "Phaedo," 49.

92 Hume, *A Treatise of Human Nature*, 252.

The idea of the self seems necessary to functioning in daily life. Even so, the nature of the self seems indeterminable—a form of placeholder nonsense. In sum, the idea of the self is necessary nonsense, an idea we are forced to entertain until something clearer comes along.

Perimortal Nonsense

Nonsense occurs in enigmatic language dying people speak while apparently transitioning into the afterlife. Some people talk cryptic nonsense during their last days, hours, and minutes of life, and when they do, it often leaves a lasting impression on witnesses. For instance, a professor of religious studies told me that her husband, a philosophy professor, talked nonsense during his final days. Even then, she said, she knew that it was nonsense, yet somewhere in the back of her mind, she felt that she somehow understood what he was saying.

Subsequently, others whose loved ones have died reported that same kind of experience to me. Furthermore, medical doctors and nurses are aware of how frequently terminally ill patients talk nonsense. Such perimortal nonsense is usually mixed in with unusual figures of speech, such as travel metaphors. Typically, medical professionals regard the enigmatic language of the dying as a manifestation of the patient's illness or the drugs administered to treat it.

Others—including doctors, nurses, and family members—have a different perspective, though, for it seems to them that the nonsensical and figurative utterances reflect transcendent experiences. Indeed, some people do seem to be on the threshold of another world as they die. They undergo a transfiguration in which their eyes brighten and their personality shines through. Witnesses sometimes remark that it seemed as though the dying person "already had one foot on the other side."

Is perimortal nonsense an involuntary response to the physiological processes of the dying brain? Or does perimortal nonsense represent deliberate attempts to verbalize ineffable transcendent experiences of transition into an afterlife realm? The theory of nonsense opens new avenues for rational investigation of these important clinical, scientific, and spiritual questions.

Dying people's final words are a topic of enduring interest and even constitute a literary genre, for numerous volumes of people's last words have been published. Such compilations tend to focus on the dying words of famous people. Furthermore, they tend to quote articulate, even eloquent, statements that are somehow representative of the dying individual's life and personality.

The process of selecting quotations for literary compilations generally winnows out nonsense. The literary compilations only include nonsense that is particularly striking or memorable. For instance, Hegel's last words were supposedly, "Only one man ever really understood me, and he didn't understand me."

Clinical experience with terminally ill patients establishes that they frequently talk nonsense. This phenomenon has not been investigated, but the theory of nonsense now provides rational means of doing so. Perimortal nonsense can be recorded, analyzed, and identified by types. Determining which rules people's nonsensical final words follow, and which rules they break, could yield insights into mental processes associated with dying.

Is perimortal nonsense a window into transcendent states of consciousness? Or, in other words, are the meaningless, unintelligible utterances of dying people sometimes instances of cross-dimensional nonsense? Earlier, we saw that the mind produces cross-dimensional nonsense when it switches between different frameworks of experience. If we can isolate definitive markers of cross-dimensional nonsense, we might be able to track the minds of the dying into the next life.

Linguist Lisa Smartt is looking at perimortal nonsense with fresh eyes. Her Final Words Project is the first systematic investigation of the phenomenon. She is collecting, analyzing, and categorizing nonsensical utterances of the dying. Her book *Words at the Threshold* (New World Library, 2017) is an important contribution to the study of death and dying. The conversation about language and the trajectory of consciousness beyond the threshold has begun.

Conclusion

I hope you have enjoyed this critical look at the tired misconceptions and erroneous assumptions about meaningless and unintelligible language, or nonsense. You've now discovered some general rational principles for guiding sound and logical thinking about nonsense. You may now even see rational principles of nonsense as a logical bridge between the questions of science and religion. An understanding of nonsense is beneficial in a plethora of ways, such as being a better writer, perceptive reader, and critical thinker. My hope is that a sort of logic of nonsense has taken shape for you, offering new perspective, and that nonsense has emerged as a delightful, thought-provoking, and useful propensity of the mind and spirit.

Bibliography

Abbott, Edwin. *Flatland: A Romance of Many Dimensions*. Boston: Roberts Brothers, 1885.

Ayer, A. J. "God-Talk Is Evidently Nonsense." *Philosophy of Religion: A Guide and Anthology*, edited by Brian Davies, 143–146. Oxford University Press, 2000.

Barrie, J. M. *Peter Pan*. London: Vintage Books, 2012.

Benham, William Gurney. *A Book of Quotations, Proverbs and Household Words*. Philadelphia: J. B. Lippincott Company, 1907.

Broad, C. D. *Lectures on Psychical Research: Incorporating the Perrott Lectures Given in Cambridge University in 1959 and 1960*. New York: Routledge, 1962.

Cannon, Edward. "An Unsuspected Fact." *A Nonsense Anthology*, edited by Carolyn Wells (New York: Charles Scribner's Sons, 1902).

Carroll, Lewis. "Alice on the Stage." *The Theatre IX* (January–June 1887): 179–184.

———. *Alice's Adventures in Wonderland*. New York: The MacMillan Company, 1920.

———. *The Hunting of the Snark: An Agony in Eight Fits*. New York: Macmillan and Company, 1899.

———. *Through the Looking-Glass and What Alice Found There*. Philadelphia: Henry Altemus Company, 1897.

———. Introduction and notes by Martin Gardner. *The Annotated Alice*. NY: Clarkson Potter, 1960.

Chesterton, G. K. *A Defense of Nonsense and Other Essays*. New York: Dodd, Mead & Company, 1911.

Clark, Katherine. *Daniel Defoe: The Whole Frame of Nature, Time and Providence*. New York: Palgrave MacMillan, 2007.

Corbet, Bishop. "Like to the Thundering Tone." *A Nonsense Anthology*, edited by Carolyn Wells, 27–28. New York: Charles Scribner's Sons, 1903.

Damrosch, Leo. *Jonathan Swift: His Life and His World*. New Haven: Yale University Press, 2013.

Derrida, Jacques. *Of Grammatology*. Translated by Gayatri Chakravorty Spivak. Baltimore: Johns Hopkins University Press, 1997.

Disney, Walt. *Pinocchio*. Directed by Ben Sharpsteen and Hamilton Luske. New York: RKO Radio Pictures, 1940.

Fowler, H. W. *A Dictionary of Modern English Usage*. United Kingdom: Wordsworth Editions, 1994.

Galton, Francis. "Thought without Words." *Nature* XXXVI (May 12, 1887): 28–29.

Hobbes, Thomas. *Leviathan*. London: Penguin Classics, 1985.

Hume, David. *Essays and Treatises on Various Subjects: With a Brief Sketch of the Author's Life and Writings*. Boston: J. P. Mendum, 1849.

———. *A Treatise of Human Nature*. Oxford: Clarendon Press, 1888.

James, William. *The Varieties of Religious Experience: A Study in Human Nature*. New York: Longmans, Green, and Co., 1903.

———. *The Will to Believe and Other Essays in Popular Philosophy*. London: Longmans, Green and Co., 1908.

Kandell, Jonathan. "Jacques Derrida, Abstruse Theorist, Dies at 74." New York Times. October 10, 2004. Accessed May 20, 2019. https://www.nytimes.com/2004/10/10/ obituaries/jacques-derrida-abstruse-theorist-dies-at-74 .html.

Keegan, Paul, ed. The Penguin Book of English *Verse. London: Penguin Books, 2004.*

Lear, Edward. "The Cummerbund." The Jumblies and Other Nonsense Verses. Oxford: Benediction Classics, 2012.

———. *The Complete Nonsense of Edward Lear.* Edited by Holbrook Jackson. New York: Dover Publications, 2012.

———. *Queery Leary Nonsense.* London: Mills & Boon, 1911.

Leoni, Edgar. *Nostradamus and His Prophecies.* Mineola: Dover Publications, 2000.

Lewis, C. S. *A Grief Observed.* United Kingdom: HarperCollins, 1996.

Lifeboat Foundation. "Advisory Board: Professor Anthony Aguirre." Accessed May 15, 2019. https://lifeboat.com /ex/bios.anthony.aguirre.

Mackay, Charles. *Memoirs of Extraordinary Popular Delusions,* Vol. I. London: Richard Bentley, 1841.

Morgenstern, Christian. "Disinternment." Translated by Jerome Lettvin. *The Fat Abbot: A Literary Review,* No. 4 (Fall–Winter, 1962): 4.

———. *Christian Morgenstern: Lullabies, Lyrics and Gallows Songs.* Anthea Bell, trans. NY: NorthSouth Books, 1995.

Nash, Ogden. "Geddondillo." *The New Yorker* (February 1, 1941): 23.

Nel, Philip. *Dr. Seuss: American Icon.* New York: Continuum, 2004.

Novella, Steven. "New Scientist on Miracles." Neurologica Blog. August 6, 2009. Accessed May 15, 2019. https://theness.com/neurologicablog/index.php/new -scientist-on-miracles/.

Parker-Pope, Tara. "Writing Your Way to Happiness." *New York Times*. January 19, 2015. Accessed May 15, 2019. https://well.blogs.nytimes.com/2015/01/19/writing -your-way-to-happiness/.

Perkowitz, Sidney. "Light Tricks: Quantum Throttling and Space-time Waves." *New Scientist*. December 14, 2011. Accessed May 15, 2019. https://www.newscientist.com /article/mg21228431-900-light-tricks-quantum -throttling-and-space-time-waves/.

Plato. "Phaedo." Translated by Hugh Tredennick. In *Plato: The Collected Dialogues*, edited by Edith Hamilton and Huntington Cairns, 40–98. Bollingen Series LXXI. Princeton: Princeton University Press, 1961.

Powell, Jason L. *Jacques Derrida: A Biography*. New York: Continuum, 2006.

Price, H. H. *Philosophical Interactions with Parapsychology: The Major Writings of H. H. Price on Parapsychology and Survival*. Edited by Frank B. Dilley. London: MacMillan, 1995.

Reynolds, Kimberley. *Radical Children's Literature: Future Visions and Aesthetic Transformations in Juvenile Fiction*. Palgrave MacMillan, 2007.

Richardson, John Anderson. *Richardson's Defense of the South*. Atlanta: A. B. Caldwell, 1914.

Sawyer, William. "Turvey Top." *The World of Wit and Humour*, edited by George Manville Fenn. London: Cassell, Petter, & Galpin, 1873.

Seuss, Dr. *I Can Lick 30 Tigers Today! and Other Stories*. New York: Random House, 1997.

Shah, Idries. *The Sufis*. London: The Idries Shah Foundation, 2015.

Shipley, Joseph T. *Dictionary of Early English*. Lanham, MD: Rowman & Littlefield Publishers, Inc., 2014.

The Supreme Yoga: Yoga Vasistha. Translated by Swami Venkatesananda. Delhi: Motilal Banarsidass, 2003.

Swinburne, Algernon Charles. "Nephelidia." *Swinburne's Poems*, edited by Arthus Beatty. New York: Thomas Y. Crowell & Co. Publishers, 1906.

Thurber, James. *Lanterns and Lances*. Philadelphia: Curtis Publishing Co., 1961.

Twain, Mark. *Mark Twain's Notebooks & Journals, Volume II (1877–1883): The Mark Twain Papers*. United Kingdom: University of California Press, 1975.

Wells, Carolyn. *A Nonsense Anthology*. New York: Charles Scribner's Sons, 1902.

Zeilberger, Doron. "Opinion 108:...The Feeling is Mutual: I Feel Sorry for Infinitarian Hugh Woodin for Feeling Sorry for Finitists Like Myself! (And the 'Lowly' Finite is MUCH More Beautiful than any 'Infinite')." Rutgers Department of Mathematics. March 16, 2010. Accessed May 15, 2019. http://sites.math.rutgers.edu/~zeilberg/Opinion108.html.

Is yellow square or round?

C. S. Lewis